Unprocess Your Life

Unprocess Your Life

BREAK FREE FROM ULTRA-PROCESSED FOODS

ROB HOBSON

Thorsons

Contents

Introduction

Our relationship with food is ever-evolving, and convenience is one of the main drivers for the most transformative shifts in how we eat. Rapid lifestyles and the need for instant gratification mean we are surrounded by choices that promise quick meals, tantalising flavours, artificially added health benefits and cheap food. This is about more than what we purchase from the local supermarket, too, as there has been a considerable increase in the amount of food delivered to or eaten out of the home, regardless of income. However, beneath the allure of convenience lies a concern: the pervasive existence of ultra-processed foods (UPFs). The nutritional characteristics of ultra-processed foods are synonymous with ill health. There is no shortage of research linking diets high in saturated fat, salt and sugar with illnesses like cardiovascular disease, high blood pressure, high cholesterol, type 2 diabetes and certain cancers, all interconnected by the overarching risk factor of being overweight or obese.

However, there is more to the story of ultra-processed foods as the complex web of additives, refined ingredients, artificial enhancements and clever product design still seems to harm health even when the nutritional components have been accounted for. This suggests that the additives in ultra-processed foods, albeit alone or combined with other factors, can potentially damage our health.

Ultra-processed foods are hyper-palatable, making them difficult to resist and easy to overconsume. A recent piece of research involving the analysis of 281 studies in 36 countries showed that one in seven people globally are addicted to ultra-processed foods, which is concerning. It's not just adults either as the study also showed one in eight children have an addiction to UPFs. These clever creations are usually vibrantly packaged and marketed in a way that entices us to purchase them. As a result, they have infiltrated our shopping baskets and kitchen cupboards to become an integral part of our daily diet. Global research has highlighted how entrenched they have become in everyday life, as in some countries such as the UK, over 50% of the foods that make it into the average shopping basket are ultra-processed. These foods are predominantly breakfast items, savoury snacks, fizzy drinks and ready meals, which comprise a third of the food purchased. In the US, Canada and the UK, as much as 80% of the energy supplied by the diet comes from ultra-processed foods.

As a nutritionist, I understand the vital role diet plays in maintaining good health, and it is second nature for me to eat well. I always pride myself on eating a balanced diet, but after delving deeper into the topic of ultra-processed foods, I was shocked at the potential effects of their additives and just how much of them were in my diet. Like everyone else, convenience sometimes influences what I eat, which may mean I grab a ready-made sandwich or 'healthy' oven-ready meal for dinner.

Then there is the squeeze of sriracha sauce on my eggs that sit on top of packaged bread, albeit a wholemeal seeded variety. I have a protein shake or bar after a workout. My wholemeal seeded bagels are filled with chicken slices and a hummus snack with wholemeal pitta bread. All these foods contain additives, which class them as ultra-processed foods.

Even though it was clear that the ingredient list was longer than it should have been to create the food I was eating, the nutritional information guided me and not the ingredients themselves. Additives like thickeners, emulsifiers and stabilizers were not a great addition to the diet. Still, I accepted that this was just part of the manufacturing process to help create these foods and not a driver for disease risk. I must also admit that the packaging and health claims made on products have influenced my food choices, so it was a revelation to learn that most foods with health claims tend to be ultra-processed.

Considering the research on ultra-processed foods, could my health be at risk even though I eat what could be viewed as a 'healthy' diet?

This book is for everyone, including those like me who unwittingly consume more ultra-processed foods than they realize and those who rely on them heavily to feed themselves. There is something in this book for everybody, and it is designed to help you plan a menu that includes many of your favourite food items you may typically purchase ready-made from the supermarket or local takeaway. The recipes have been structured to satisfy all those moments when we are most vulnerable to ultra-processed foods, such as dinnertime with the kids, quick meals and packed lunches. This book also teaches you the skills you need to understand and approach food in a more organized way of batch-cooking, freezing and avoiding waste to make living an unprocessed life an achievable reality.

There is something deeply satisfying about becoming self-sufficient with your food. Please share my passion and experience of what this feels like by living an unprocessed life. Toasting a slice of your own home-baked bread and slathering it with homemade nut butter, topping it with scrambled eggs and homemade sriracha or making a Thai green curry with your own freshly made coconut milk is just a couple of my most satisfying food moments. You can also share these moments with others: homecooked Chicken tikka masala (see page 84) and Wholemeal pitta breads (see page 194) with your family for curry night or making your kids the best-tasting crispy Fish fingers (see page 125) or Bashed seeded chicken (see page 126) with a squeeze of homemade Tomato ketchup (see page 199), which beats the slightly disappointing food moment of overly flavoured and undoubtedly nutritionally poor ultra-processed versions.

This is not just a cookbook but a handbook to help guide you on your journey to living a healthy life free of ultra-processed foods.

What are ultra-processed foods?

There is no agreed definition of an ultra-processed food. Still, they typically have five or more ingredients and can't be created at home. They include many additives and ingredients not used in home cooking, such as preservatives, emulsifiers, sweeteners, artificial colours and flavours. These foods generally have a long shelf life. They are manufactured to be convenient, cheap and hyper-palatable, so you want to eat more of them. The term 'ultra-processed' was coined by researchers to help distinguish between less processed and minimally processed foods. Carlos Monteiro and his research team at the University of São Paulo in Brazil developed the most widely acknowledged classification of foods by their level of processing. Research in this area led to the NOVA classification system, which classifies foods into four groups depending on their degree of processing. NOVA is the Portuguese word for 'new' and this is a brand new way of classifying food and a relatively modern concept.

The NOVA system has been widely used in research but comes with criticism. Some argue that the system needs to be simplified and consider the full complexity of food processing, as foods are grouped into broad categories without consideration for their specific nutritional profiles. A good example is wholemeal bread and very sugary breakfast cereals, which feature in the same category regardless of the differences between them nutritionally. Along the same lines, focusing on the extent of processing does not account for the nutrient content of foods, meaning certain processed foods that are nutritionally poor may be classed as being 'healthier' because they are not ultra-processed such as sugared or salted nuts, cured meats or fruit canned in syrup.

Regardless of the arguments, the NOVA system has helped to establish a link between diets high in ultra-processed foods and an increased risk of disease, so the fact remains that foods that fall into this category are harming our health.

The NOVA system (abbreviated from the Food and Agriculture Organization of the United Nations, 2019)

NOVA 1 – UNPROCESSED OR MINIMALLY PROCESSED FOODS

Edible parts of plants (fruit, seeds, leaves, stems, roots, tubers) or from animals (muscle, fat, offal, eggs, milk), fungi (mushrooms) and algae after harvesting.

Unprocessed foods that have undergone a process that is common in a household kitchen, such as the removal of inedible parts, drying, powdering, crushing, grinding, chilling, freezing, poaching, boiling, placing in containers, vacuum packing, fermentation (non-alcoholic) and other methods that do not add salt, sugar, oils or fats, or other substances to the original food. These processes are done to extend the life of unprocessed foods so they can be stored for more extended use, made edible and make their preparation easier or more diverse.

Occasionally, minimally processed foods contain additives that prolong product duration, protect original properties or prevent microorganisms from growing on them.

UNPROCESSED OR MINIMALLY PROCESSED FOODS

- Freshly squeezed, chilled, frozen or dried fruit, and leafy and root vegetables.
- Grains including brown, parboiled or white rice, barley, corn cob and kernel.
- Legumes such as beans, lentils and chickpeas (dried or tinned in water).
- Starchy root vegetables and tubers including potatoes, sweet potatoes and cassava.
- Fresh or dried mushrooms.
- Meat, poultry, fish and seafood, whole or as steaks, fillets and other cuts.
- Fresh, powdered*, chilled or frozen eggs.
- Fresh, powdered* or pasteurized milk.
- Fresh or pasteurized fruit and vegetable juices (no added sugar, sweeteners or flavouring).
- Flour made from corn, cassava or grains such as wheat and spelt.
- Nuts and seeds (no added salt, sugar or flavourings).
- Herbs and spices used to cook including fresh, whole, powdered or dried.
- Fresh or pasteurized natural yoghurt.
- Tea, coffee and drinking water.

Also include foods made up from two or more of the items in this group including:

- Dried mixed fruits and nuts.
- Pasta, couscous and polenta made with flour and water.
- Foods with vitamins and minerals added to replace those lost during processing such as wheat flour fortified with iron, calcium and vitamins B1 (thiamine) and B3 (niacin).

* Powdered eggs and milk are only classed as NOVA group 1 if nothing has been added.

NOVA 2 – PROCESSED CULINARY INGREDIENTS

These are foods from NOVA group 1 or from nature obtained by industrial processes such as pressing, refining, extracting or mining. Such ingredients are used to prepare, season and cook foods from group 1. They may contain additives that prolong the ingredient's shelf life, protect the original properties or prevent microorganisms from growing on them.

PROCESSED CULINARY INGREDIENTS

- Vegetable oils crushed from seeds, nuts and fruit (olives).
- Butter and lard sourced from milk and pork.
- Sugar and molasses obtained from cane or beet.
- Honey extracted from combs and syrup from maple trees.
- Starches extracted from plants such as corn (cornflour).
- Salt mined or sourced from seawater and table salt with added drying agents.

Also includes foods made up from two or more of the items in this group such as salted butter or with added vitamins and minerals such as iodised salt.

What are ultra-processed foods?

NOVA 3 – PROCESSED FOODS

Foods made by adding salt, oil, sugar or other processed culinary ingredients from NOVA group 2 to foods from group 1 (unprocessed and minimally processed), using preservation methods such as canning, bottling and in the case of bread and cheese, using fermentation (non-alcoholic). The processes and ingredients used here are designed to increase the durability of group 1 foods and make them more enjoyable by modifying or enhancing their sensory qualities. These foods may contain additives that prolong their shelf life, protect original properties or prevent microorganisms from growing on them.

PROCESSED FOODS

- Canned and bottled vegetables and legumes in brine.
- Salted or sugared nuts and seeds.
- Salted, dried, cured or smoked meats and fish.
- Canned fish (with or without preservatives).
- Pickled or fermented vegetables and fruit in syrup (with or without added antioxidants – ascorbic acid also known as vitamin C).
- Freshly made unpackaged bread and cheese.
- Wine, cider and beer.

NOVA 4 – ULTRA-PROCESSED FOODS

Formulation of ingredients made by a series of industrial processes, many requiring specialist sophisticated equipment and technology. These processes include fractioning whole foods into substances, chemical modification of such substances, and assembly of unmodified and modified food substances using industrial techniques like moulding and pre-frying. Additives are also used at various manufacturing stages to make the final food product palatable or hyper-palatable.

Aside from adding sugar, oils, fats and salt in combination, other substances of no or rare culinary use are added, such as high-fructose corn syrup, hydrogenated fats and protein isolates.

These foods contain additives that prolong their shelf life, protect their original properties, provide palatability and more appealing flavours, or prevent microorganisms from growing on them, such as flavour enhancers, emulsifiers, sweeteners, thickeners, colourings, and bulking, foaming, gelling and glazing agents.

ULTRA-PROCESSED FOODS

An abundance of ready-to-eat products including:

- Carbonated soft drinks.
- Sweet or savoury packaged snacks.
- Chocolate and confectionary (sweets).
- Ice cream.
- Mass-produced packaged breads and buns.
- Margarines and other spreads.
- Cookies (biscuits), pastries, cakes and cake mixes.
- Breakfast 'cereals', 'cereal' and 'energy' bars.
- 'Energy' drinks.
- Milk drinks, 'fruit' yoghurts and 'fruit' drinks.
- 'Cocoa' drinks.
- 'Instant' sauces.
- Pies, pasta and pizza dishes.
- Poultry and fish 'nuggets' and 'sticks', sausages, burgers, hot dogs and other reconstituted meat products.
- Powdered and packaged 'instant' soups, noodles and desserts.
- Products designed for 'health' and 'slimming' such as meal replacement shakes and protein powders.
- Spirits including vodka, gin, whiskey and rum.

What additives are used to manufacture ultra-processed foods?

____

Food additives, such as salt, sugar or sulphur dioxide, have been used for centuries to preserve food. However, to meet the needs of the food industry and produce food on a large scale, additives have been developed to ensure that processed food remains safe and in good condition from the factory it is made to wherever it ends up.

Many food additives are found in ultra-processed foods, and they are added at several different stages of production, including processing, manufacturing and packaging. The purpose of these substances is to improve the sensory properties of the food, nutritional value or shelf life. Improved texture and mouthfeel can be achieved by adding a thickener. At the same time, taste can be enhanced with additives that mimic natural flavours, and artificial colouring can prevent the product fading over time. As well as making sure the quality of the food remains consistent, additives are also used to help ensure the safety of a food product by preventing the growth of microbes.

The use of additives helps manufacturers meet the demands of consumers looking for convenient, tasty and attractive food. From a manufacturing perspective, they are needed in the processing of food. Additives are also used in food to mimic more expensive components, which helps to reduce the cost of ultra-processed foods for the consumer but increases the profits for the food industry. This may involve adding artificial flavours instead of natural fruit, spices or herbs; sweeteners like high-fructose corn syrup as an alternative to sugar in snacks, puddings and desserts; or thickening and gelling agents to replace ingredients like cream, eggs or purées to make sauces and puddings.

While the research looking at specific individual additives and health is as of yet scant, we do know that whether alone or in combination with other factors, these compounds do not positively affect our health.

Flavour enhancers

These ingredients are added to foods to improve their taste and palatability, as ultra-processed foods lack the natural flavour of whole or minimally processed foods. Flavour enhancers can also provide consistency in taste, extend the flavour across the shelf life and mask undesirable tastes. These additives can also encourage overeating, stimulating taste receptors and making food more addictive.

Monosodium glutamate (MSG), disodium inosinate, disodium guanylate, hydrolysed vegetable protein (HVP), autolysed yeast extract, ethyl maltol, methyl anthranilate, butyric acid, diacetyl, and artificial fruit flavours designed to replicate natural fruits.

Emulsifiers

Different types of emulsifiers are added to ultra-processed foods for several reasons. Emulsifiers help to improve the texture of food (smooth and creamy), prevent ingredients from settling or splitting, reduce the fat content, improve mouthfeel, increase shelf life, and help to evenly disperse flavours within a food product.

Lecithin, mono- and diglycerides, polysorbates (including polysorbate 80), soy lecithin, sodium stearoyl lactylate, microcrystalline cellulose, carboxymethylcellulose.

Sweeteners

These ingredients are added to ultra-processed foods to enhance their sweetness and improve the flavour and palatability of the product. Sweeteners also include artificial varieties which are calorie-free and chemical in nature.

High-fructose corn syrup (HFCS), inverted glucose syrup, sucrose, aspartame, saccharin, acesulfame potassium, sucralose, steviol glycosides (stevia), sugar alcohols also known as polyols which include sorbitol, isomalt, erythritol.

Thickeners and stabilizers

These are added to ultra-processed foods to help improve the texture and stability of foods while maintaining the quality and shelf life. Thickeners and stabilizers contribute to the appearance of food (preventing settling and clumping), provide a better mouthfeel (thicker and more substantial texture), prevent separation, and improve the freeze-thaw stability in foods like ice cream.

Modified starches (corn, tapioca, and potato), xanthan gum, guar gum, carrageenan, pectin, cellulose gum, locust bean gum (carob gum), konjac gum, Arabic gum (acacia gum).

Preservatives

There are several reasons why preservatives are added to ultra-processed foods. Still, primarily, it is to extend their shelf life and ensure that, over time, their flavour, texture and appearance are maintained. Adding preservatives to food helps to prevent the growth of microbes and product deterioration, which can occur because of exposure to air, light and fluctuations in temperature.

Sodium benzoate, potassium sorbate, calcium propionate, sodium nitrite, sodium nitrate, sulphites butylated hydroxyanisole, calcium propionate, sodium propionate, ascorbic acid (vitamin C).

Bulking agents

Bulking agents are also known as fillers and are added to ultra-processed foods to increase the volume of a food product, making it appear more substantial. These agents also help to improve texture and mouthfeel, reduce the calorie, fat or sugar content by replacing certain ingredients and allow the manufacturer to reduce the overall cost of producing their product.

Maltodextrin, polydextrose, inulin, cellulose, psyllium husk, oat fibre, wheat protein isolate, soy protein isolate, whey protein isolate, chicory root powder.

Artificial colourings

These additives are added to ultra-processed foods to enhance the visual appearance of a food product. This is important to manufacturers for several reasons, as they help to differentiate and provide consistency between products, mask unattractive colours, act as visual cues for flavour and contribute to brand identity.

Sunset yellow (E110), quinoline yellow (E104), carmoisine (E122), Allura red (E129), tartrazine (E102), brilliant blue (E133), indigo carmine (E132), patent blue V (E131).

How to identify an ultra-processed food

Living a life utterly free of ultra-processed food may only be achievable sometimes, and this may not be through personal choice, as food access, especially when you are away from home, can make things tricky. Even when trying to follow a healthy, balanced diet, there are still ultra-processed choices on 'healthy' ready-prepared meals, snacks and everyday essentials.

You don't need to analyze the packet of every food you eat. The foods classed as NOVA 1 and 2 are obviously not ultra-processed, such as fruits, vegetables, milk, fresh meat, poultry and fish. When you get to manufactured food items such as breakfast cereals, bread, yoghurt, spreads, dressings and sauces, it becomes unclear.

There are many examples of how food goes from unprocessed or minimally processed to ultra-processed, and a good example is bread. Traditionally made bread is created by combining wheat flour, water, salt and yeast, making it a processed food but a healthy dietary staple. Bread becomes ultra-processed when you add emulsifiers, preservatives and other such additives that can extend its shelf life by 10–14 days.

Snacks are significantly associated with the consumption of ultra-processed foods. While there is nothing wrong with snacking or, in fact, eating the occasional ultra-processed food now and then as a treat, they are not all created equally. I think a valuable point to make here is that there is a risk that the NOVA system could start demonizing foods when, in fact, there should be no 'bad' or 'good' but just a shift of focus towards eating more of the foods that are better for our health and limiting others to occasional eating.

Unprocessed or minimally processed	Processed	Ultra-processed
Puffed wheat (nothing added)	Shredded wheat	Shreddies (contains invert sugar syrup and barley malt extract)
Oats	Granola (sugar free with nothing but raw whole food ingredients)	Oat cereal with added chocolate
Freshly squeezed orange juice	Sweetened fruit juice	Fruit-flavoured drink with artificial colours and flavourings
Home roasted chicken	Deli rotisserie chicken	Fried chicken (takeaway)
Whole potatoes	Fresh mashed potato	Instant mashed potato
Wholegrain crackers (minimal ingredient list)	Naturally flavoured wholegrain crackers (salt, pepper, dried herbs)	Artificially flavoured crackers
Tortilla chips made using home-made wholemeal tortilla	Plain tortilla crisps	Artificially flavoured tortilla crisps (Dorritos)

Even within the ultra-processed food category, the difference between the same kinds of foods is quite extreme, and a good example is crisps. A premium branded salted crisp is better than a Pringle, which contains no real potato and is glued together with different flours and emulsifiers, and is artificially coloured. You may also find the Pringle more addictive as it has been engineered to be hyper-palatable. The shape fits perfectly into your mouth and onto your tongue with an explosion of flavour before it crunches and slowly dissolves. The easy-to-open and portable design of the tube makes them even easier to open, reseal and carry around, while the design also leaves you with the perception you are not eating as much as you are.

The same kind of food and, in fact, the very same food can also span different categories, which can

PREMIUM BRANDED SALTED CRISPS

Ingredients: Potatoes, sunflower oil, salt.

PRINGLES ORIGINAL

Ingredients: Dehydrated potatoes, vegetable oils (sunflower, palm, corn) in varying proportions, wheat flour, corn flour, rice flour, maltodextrin, emulsifier (E471), salt, colour (annatto norbixin).

How to identify an ultra-processed food

make messaging around ultra-processed foods very confusing. Peanut butter, for example, can fall into NOVA 1 if made purely from raw nuts. It moves into NOVA 2 if you add salt, sugar or oil. It becomes ultra-processed when a preservative or other artificial additive is used. The same is true of yoghurt, a protein and calcium source in many people's diets. Still, it becomes ultra-processed once you flavour or artificially sweeten it and add thickeners to make it virtually fat-free. In these instances, I suggest finding your brand and sticking to it to make it easier to do your weekly unprocessed food shop for foods you are not making yourself at home.

Another interesting take on this topic of reading the label is foods that are sold to us as a healthy alternative when, in fact, they are much more ultra-processed than the original food they are meant to be replacing. Plant-based milk is the perfect example and is derived from various nuts, coconut, legumes (soy), grains and seeds to replace dairy milk. They are designed to alleviate consumer fears over allergies, lactose intolerance, inflammation, antibiotics, pesticides and hormones. They are viewed as healthier by the consumer either because of a food trend or the influence of marketing and social media.

Plant-based milk is needed by some people as an alternative solution to dairy milk as they have lactose intolerance, but this affects fewer people than you would think, with only around 8% of the UK population being affected, for example.

Some brands also use other processes to achieve a smoother-tasting drink, like oat milk manufacturers that use natural digestive enzymes such as alpha-amylase to break down the starch into simple sugars such as maltose to give a smoother-tasting product (although this does not factor into the ultra-processed conversation).

A study from the United States in 2021 explored the topic of plant-based milk and found that many of them met the criteria for an ultra-processed food. It found that 69% of the milk reviewed contained added salt while 53% had added sugars, and most contained stabilizers and emulsifiers to keep the product from splitting, and thickening substances (gums) to improve palatability and mimic the mouthfeel and creaminess of the original product (dairy milk).

Like everything in life, you get what you pay for. There are better quality brands that produce plant milk with minimal processing, which contains just water, oats, nuts or seeds and sea salt. Still, of course, they come at a premium. Even cheaper is to try making it yourself, and you can find recipes for coconut, nut and oat milk in the section on sauces, dressings and milk.

BRANDED OAT MILK DRINK

Water, oats (9%), sunflower oil, chicory root fibre, maltodextrin, tricalcium, phosphate, sea salt, stabilizer: gellan gum, vitamins B12, B2 and D2.

BRANDED HEMP SEED MILK

Water, hemp seed base (4%), acidity regulator (dipotassium phosphate), emulsifier (sunflower lecithin), stabilizer (gellan gum), sea salt.

BRANDED MINIMALLY PROCESSED ALMOND MILK

Spring water, organic almonds 5% and sea salt.

Positive health messaging has also driven the popularity of ultra-processed plant-based food products. Going plant-based is undoubtedly good for your health. Still, it is just as easy to become an unhealthy vegan nowadays. When veganism became a food and diet trend, the market responded by producing convenience food that made it easier to follow this way of eating. This evolved into plant-based eating, and now the market shelves are flooded with 'alternative' food items. These items are worth checking the label on as, ironically, a diet that should be driven by the consumption of whole, unprocessed foods such as beans, pulses, lentils, nuts, seeds and tofu is now dominated by ready-prepared and often like-for-like products with oxymoronic names such as plant-based bacon and vegan chicken chunks. To produce these foods, they often rely on additives such as modified starches, artificial colourings, stabilizers and thickeners, usually in gums.

Snacks are another place you need to pay attention to the ingredient label. Visit any supermarket website and search under their healthy snacks section. It will be full of ultra-processed foods, many of which parents buy for their kids. Sweet snacks are wildly misleading, including protein and energy bars, breakfast bars, snack pots and yoghurt-covered dried fruit. Many of these products are marketed as healthy options, and the situation is helped along by clever advertising, desirable packaging and a smattering of health claims.

Interestingly, if a food has a health claim, it is often ultra-processed. In this category, we have snacks like 'high in protein' flavoured chicken pieces, 'baked not fried' flavoured rice crackers and 'rich in calcium' processed cheese spread with savoury crackers 'dunkers'. I even found one 'high in fibre' flapjack that contained 20 ingredients, including two types of oil, three types of sugar,

emulsifiers, stabilizers and chicory root fibre used as a source of inulin, undoubtedly added to help achieve the high fibre health claim. The bottom line is don't believe everything you read on the front cover!

Sometimes, when choosing a daily food, there may be only a minimally processed version if you make it yourself. This is the case with one of the most used condiments worldwide, tomato ketchup. Again, this is about looking at the label to see what is in the product and making the best choice depending on what is used in the formulation. On paper, the Heinz ketchup doesn't look that bad. It is free of artificial colourings, flavourings, preservatives and thickeners. Still, it contains a lot of added sugar, and I do not know what the spice and herb extracts involve.

HEINZ TOMATO KETCHUP

Tomatoes (148g per 100g tomato ketchup), spirit vinegar, sugar, salt, spice, and herb extracts (contain celery), spice.

SUPERMARKET OWN BRAND OF TOMATO KETCHUP

Water, tomato purée (29%), sugar, spirit vinegar, maize starch, salt, spice blend (salt, tomato powder, clove extract), and clove leaf oil.

How to identify an ultra-processed food

How do ultra-processed foods affect your health?

I have already touched on the fact that in many countries, ultra-processed foods make up a significant part of the average shopping basket and contribute to a high percentage of the energy consumed by some people. This increased consumption of ultra-processed foods also influences the overall energy intake of the diet, as well as salt, saturated fats and sugar.

The more ultra-processed foods you eat, the more calories you are likely to consume alongside higher amounts of saturated fat, sugar and salt. These diet components are all associated with an increased risk of non-communicable diseases such as cardiovascular disease, type 2 diabetes and cancer when eaten in excess, and increased inflammation in the body, which underlies all these diseases. The tendency of ultra-processed food to foster overconsumption is also why they are linked to disease risk. High intake of these nutrients can also increase the chances of developing other conditions that are risk factors for non-communicable diseases such as high blood pressure, high cholesterol, overweight and obesity.

Studies have also shown that the more ultra-processed food you eat, the less fibre and other vital vitamins, minerals and plant compounds that protect health and disease risk you consume.

Food processing also influences how our body responds to it, as the food matrix is altered. This can affect satiety, nutrient availability, and the speed at which food is digested and assimilated into the body. When nuts are eaten whole, the body absorbs less of the fat than when they are ground down into an oil. When fruits are turned into a juice or juice drink, they significantly

Thinly sliced and uniform creates a light crisp texture with a consistent crunch and feel.

Deep-frying creates a satisfactory crisp texture, rich in flavour and golden colour. The way they melt in the mouth adds to their moreish mouthfeel.

Additives and flavourings are carefully formulated to create a taste sensation that is hard to resist.

The aroma of freshly cooked crisps is designed to stimulate the senses and increase the enjoyment of eating, contributing to their addictive nature.

Marketing and branding strategies help to create emotional connections with production such as enjoyment, relaxation and socialising.

Adding salt helps to trigger reward centres in the brain making eating pleasurable. In combination with carbohydrates and fat, crisps become hard to resist.

influence blood sugar levels as the fibre is removed. When a piece of pork is turned into an ultra-processed piece of bacon or sausage with additives such as nitrate and nitrates, it carries an increased risk of cancer due to the compounds that form when it is cooked. This risk is supported by strong evidence reviewed by the World Cancer Research Fund.

How your body reacts to food processing can also go the other way and be of benefit. When you process tomatoes into a can or purée, the antioxidant lycopene (responsible for the fruit's red colour) becomes more bioavailable in the body, allowing you to absorb more of it.

Ultra-processing makes foods hyper-palatable, meaning they are hard to resist eating. This does not happen by accident, as many foods are engineered to become almost addictive. Crisps are an excellent example, as the simple potato would never be called an addictively good food. Still, once you have converted it to an ultra-processed food by cutting it in a specific way, flavouring it and then marketing it in a certain way, it is a whole different story.

The link between a nutritionally poor diet and the risk of disease is well established, and it is widely recommended that people follow an anti-inflammatory diet such as the Mediterranean diet to maintain good health. But this is where things get interesting; many of the studies in this area have adjusted their findings to account for the saturated fat, salt and sugar in ultra-processed foods, suggesting something else about these foods is putting your health at risk.

A review of 43 studies carried out in 2020 found at least one adverse health outcome associated with the consumption of ultra-processed food in 37 of these research papers. These adverse health outcomes included obesity, overweight, cancer, type 2 diabetes, cardiovascular diseases (heart disease and stroke), IBS, depression, and frailty conditions such as poor bone and muscle health.

A study of nearly 20,000 Spanish graduates carried out in 2019 found that the group of people eating the greatest amount of ultra-processed food (more than four servings daily) were 62% more likely to have died after an average of 10 years than the people eating the least amount (less than two servings daily). It was also found that the risk of dying was increased by 18% for each additional serving.

Ultra-processed foods and cardiovascular disease

Cardiovascular diseases are the leading cause of death globally, and these are conditions that affect the heart and blood vessels, including heart disease, heart attack, hypertension, stroke and vascular dementia.

A study of more than 100,000 French adults in 2019 followed their diet over five years and found that eating more ultra-processed foods was linked to a greater risk of heart disease. It was found that a 10% increase in ultra-processed foods led to a 12% increase in cases of heart and circulatory diseases. Two recent studies (2023) found similar links to cardiovascular disease. Still, what makes them so relevant is after adjusting the findings for saturated fat, salt and sugar, the conclusions remained the same, suggesting that something in the processing of the food is causing the risk.

One of these studies, carried out by the Fourth Medical Military University in China, involved pooled data from 325,000 people who were then divided into four groups depending on their daily intake of ultra-processed food. Those with the highest intakes of ultra-processed foods were 24% more likely to develop heart disease or suffer a stroke or heart attack. Furthermore, for every 10% increase in the proportion of ultra-processed foods, there was a 6% increase in heart disease risk. This notion of 'the more you eat, the greater the risk' is common in all studies linking ultra-processed foods to poor health.

The second of these studies, carried out by researchers at the University of Sydney, followed 10,000 middle-aged women for 15 years and recorded what they ate. Those who ate the most ultra-processed foods were 39% more likely to develop high blood pressure, significantly increasing their heart attack and stroke risk.

Adverse Health Outcomes

There are several routes that ultra-processed foods can impact on our health outcomes, and these are often overlapping

JUNK FOOD
Ultra-processed foods are usually high in saturated fat, sugar and salt which can increase your risk factors for disease

EATING HABITS
Ultra-processed foods are hyper-palatable, convenient, and marketed in a way that encourages mindless eating during distractive activites. This can encourage snacking, rushed eating and over consumption

DISPLACEMENT
The more ultra-processed the food you eat the less fresh and nutritious food gets included in your diet. Research shows this is more prevalent amongst those with lower incomes

APPETITE
Consuming ultra-processed foods has been shown to disrupt satiety signalling, which tells us we are full after eating. This is mediated by the gut microbiome, hormone and digestive system. These foods can encourage compulsive eating

FOOD QUALITY
The ultra-processing of food has changed the quality of everyday essentials that we buy, such as bread and breakfast cereal depleting them of beneficial nutrients and pushing them into the category of junk food

GUT MICROBIOME
Diets rich in ultra-processed foods usually lack the variety and fibre, which can lead to alterations in the gut microbiome. Additives can also impact on the diversity of bacteria in the gut, affecting digestion and the uptake of nutrients from food

Dementia is a worrying concern for everyone as they age, as is the decline in cognition, a term used to describe the mental processes in the brain, including thinking, language, learning and memory. There may be a link between ultra-processed foods and dementia and cognitive decline.

A study in the journal Neurology in 2022 involving over 72,000 people found that a 10% increase in ultra-processed food consumption raised the risk of all-cause dementia by 10%. Interestingly, this study also showed that replacing 10% of the ultra-processed foods in the diet with unprocessed or minimally processed foods was estimated to be associated with a 19% lower risk of dementia. Similar findings have also shown how higher intakes of ultra-processed foods may be linked to a faster rate of cognitive decline among older people.

Ultra-processed foods and obesity

The link between obesity and ultra-processed foods is interesting and one of the first areas where additives in food were suspected of playing a role in poor health. One of the most fascinating and pivotal studies frequently quoted in the conversation about ultra-processed foods investigated the impact different diets had on body weight with or without ultra-processed foods.

This study carried out in 2019 took two groups of men and fed them an ultra-processed diet for two weeks, then a non-ultra-processed diet for two weeks, and they could eat as much as they liked. The food provided was matched nutritionally, but during the ultra-processed diet, they consumed an average of 508 calories more than when exposed to the unprocessed diet. They also gained

an average of 0.9kg during the ultra-processed diet. Still, they lost an average of 0.9kg during the non-ultra-processed diet. This study suggests that ultra-processed foods lead to overeating but that it is something other than the nutrients in the food causing people to gain weight.

Ultra-processed foods and type 2 diabetes

A large ongoing study in France based on the NutriNet-santé cohort has identified a significant direct association between the amount of ultra-processed foods in the diet and the incidence of type 2 diabetes even after controlling for saturated fat, salt, sugar and fibre intakes. Further research involving this same cohort suggested that dietary nitrates, such as those found in ultra-processed meats, may play a role in the condition. A similar study published in the Journal of International Epidemiology also found that compared to non-consumption of ultra-processed foods, moderate intake increased the risk of diabetes by 12%.

Ultra-processed foods and cancer

Research has also implicated that there may be a link between ultra-processed foods and certain types of cancer. The French NutriNet-santé study has found that after adjusting for other factors that may put you at risk of cancer, there are significant direct associations between overall and, more specifically, breast cancer. A 10% increase in the proportion of ultra-processed food in the diet was shown to significantly increase this cancer risk by more than 10%.

Ultra-processed foods and the microbiome

New theories are also intimating that ultra-processed foods have a significant effect on your gut health. This exciting area of nutrition research is starting to unveil the many ways our gut is fundamental to health concerning mental health, weight maintenance, immunity, hormone regulation, and its role in digestion and energy metabolism.

Studies have shown how additives added to ultra-processed foods can affect the functioning of the gut microbiome, which is the diverse collection of microorganisms that inhabit your gastrointestinal tract. While they do not prove cause and effect, they contribute to the growing evidence suggesting that ultra-processed foods negatively affect the microbiome and health.

Animal studies have shown that emulsifiers in many ultra-processed foods can affect the gut. Two specific emulsifiers called carboxymethylcellulose and polysorbate 80 were found to reduce the diversity of bacteria in mice. We know from research in humans that reduced microbial diversity is associated with poor health outcomes, including obesity and type 2 diabetes. Emulsifiers have also been shown to enhance gut inflammation by impacting microbiota composition and functionality. It has also been suggested that the additives in food could interact with the gut, affecting the digestive process and uptake of nutrients from the food we eat. Artificial sweeteners may also have an impact and could be one of the factors linking ultra-processed foods to a higher risk of obesity and type 2 diabetes. Sweeteners such as aspartame have been shown to impact insulin resistance, affecting how sugar is absorbed into the bloodstream.

Research has highlighted, the difference between the diversity of bacteria in the gut of obese people compared to those with a healthy weight and the type of food they eat is likely to play a role in this. Higher intakes of ultra-processed foods have also been associated with an increased risk of irritable bowel syndrome (IBS) and functional dyspepsia.

The research in this area is new and evolving to help us understand whether it is one of many different factors that are harming our health. It is also difficult to know whether it is something within ultra-processed foods causing issues or whether eating a diet high in these foods suggests an overall lifestyle linked to poorer health.

It is important to note that all the studies in this area are observational, meaning they can only show associations and not prove a definitive cause and effect between ultra-processed food intake and adverse health outcomes. There is also a need for more research to identify individual additives in ultra-processed foods and health outcomes.

It is also easy to cherry-pick research findings. Still, the research has a generally similar pattern of study findings. While the evidence still needs strengthening to establish a causal link between ultra-processed food and adverse health outcomes, the research is rapidly accumulating. Considering this, it is fair to say that consuming these foods in large amounts offers no beneficial effects; instead, they are associated with various adverse health outcomes, so it seems sensible to try and cut down on the amount you eat.

How to use this book

_____

The layout of this cookbook is designed to make it easier for you to embark on your journey to living an unprocessed life. It's not just about recipes but the tools you need to save kitchen time to create unprocessed convenience food rather than reaching for something ready-made and ultra-processed.

The information in the following chapters will show you how to approach this new way of eating and preparing food. You will be guided through the basic principles of unprocessed living and shown how to overcome some of the hurdles you may come up against on your way. I will also answer some of the most commonly asked questions about living an unprocessed life and help you understand how to freeze and batch-cook food properly, which can save you pounds on your food bill and minimise food waste.

We make food choices for many reasons, including taste, social influences, dietary preferences, convenience, availability, emotion and cost. All of these can influence our decision to choose an ultra-processed food. The recipes in this book have been designed to offer you a healthier, unprocessed version of some of your ultra-processed favourites so you can make healthier food choices.

Navigating the recipes

___

The recipe section of this book has been organized into meal occasions that will help you to fit mealtimes around your personal lifestyle. These are moments during the day when stress, time constraints, having to work and eat from the

office, or generally feeling like you can't face cooking lead us to reach for something ultra-processed. There are recipes in this book for quick evening meals, feeding the kids, packed lunches, snacking and other occasions for you to explore and get familiar with.

One of the key sections of this book is the sauces, dressings and milk. This section contains recipes to help you create many ultra-processed store cupboard essentials that make their way into your shopping basket every week. These include tomato ketchup, chilli sauce, plant-based milks, jarred sauces and salad dressings. This is an excellent place to start your journey to create some commonly used ingredients you can batch-cook and keep in store. To make things easier, many of the dressings and sauces in this section appear in different recipes throughout the book, and they can be adapted to suit the dishes you are cooking. The versatile red pepper sauce and basic tomato sauce are two perfect examples of recipes you can adapt to make your own, and you can always have a few batches of them in your freezer. Over time, you may find other recipes that you can use to continue your unprocessed life beyond this book.

COOKING TIPS AND SERVING SUGGESTIONS

At the end of most recipes in this book, you will find advice on how to freeze the food, and in the subsequent chapters, I will explain the best and safest way to do this so you retain the quality of the food. You will also find tips to help you adapt recipes or serve the dish differently so the recipes work a little harder for you.

Using leftovers

Making good use of leftovers and batch-cooked food is integral to living an unprocessed life. If you have anything left over in the fridge, there is always a new way to use it. I have stuffed homemade pitta bread with leftovers such as the Middle Eastern style aubergine stew, turkey meatballs and red pepper sauce. The bashed-seeded chicken has also made its way into a bread roll with a big dollop of tomato ketchup or sriracha many times!

If you have any leftover sauces, dressings or milk, try looking for recipes in the book that use them, as many are used multiple times. This is a great way to help keep your fridge free of odd pots of food and avoid food wastage.

Meal planning

Being prepared can also help you on your journey to living an unprocessed life, including meal planning. Really think about how your week looks before deciding the recipes you want to cook. Do you have a busy week and need to pick quick meals? You must start work early, then you may decide to cook something for dinner that can be taken into work the following day for lunch or batch-cook some of the lunch recipes from the book. Would it be helpful to batch-cook some protein energy bars to take to work each day or eat after your early morning workout sessions if you know grabbing breakfast immediately afterwards could be a struggle? This book is about providing solutions to help you meet the needs of your daily lifestyle.

Sourcing ingredients

There is little point pretending that cooking from scratch will be cheaper than a trolley full of £1 frozen ready meals, but there are ways to eat that can make it much more cost-effective than you think. Some of the recipes in this book are also cheaper to prepare than others, so you may want to consider this when planning what meals to prepare or batch-cook across the week. These recipes tend to be plant-based or use different cuts of meat, such as chicken thigh over breast.

I have already spoken about batch-cooking and freezing dishes, which will save you money in their preparation and influence your decision to order something in or eat out when you have dishes prepared in your freezer or fridge. You can also shop around for ingredients rather than relying on one supermarket. There are always deals to be had in health food shops or online when bulk buying certain dry foods like nuts, seeds, dried fruits, lentils, legumes and processed cooking ingredients. You can also look for frozen meat, poultry, fish and seafood varieties, as freezing means it remains in the NOVA 1 category.

How to live an unprocessed life

This book is intended to help you reduce the ultra-processed food you eat in your diet. How to live an unprocessed life should be seen as a lifestyle shift and not a 'flash in the pan' health kick. How far you decide to take this is up to you, but I suggest small steps for long-term success. These small changes will quickly become second nature as you slowly change how you eat.

The foods used in the recipes that follow are unprocessed or minimally processed. To save time, there are also options to include 'healthy' processed foods like canned legumes or a loaf of good-quality fresh bread from a baker, as sometimes you may not have the time or the patience to soak or bake your own. There is nothing wrong with this, as part of living an unprocessed life is being realistic about what you feel you are willing and able to do to achieve long-term success in reducing your ultra-processed food intake.

I had never thought about making my own coconut milk. Still, once I understood how to do it and freeze it in bulk, I never thought twice when planning a curry or dahl for dinner. The same applies to tomato ketchup and sriracha sauce, two commonly used condiments in my kitchen. Before my own journey to living an unprocessed life, I had never really batch-cooked and frozen food, but this has now become something I do weekly. It is a godsend after a tiring day to know I have something I can reheat, so I have more time to do other things to help me unwind and relax.

These are unprocessed wins, and after embarking on this mission to live an unprocessed life, many more have now become instinctive.

Prioritize whole foods

This approach is fundamental to living an unprocessed life. These foods are free of ultra-processing and have a much higher nutrient density, meaning they are richer in vitamins, minerals, phytonutrients (beneficial plant compounds) and fibre, which help the body to function correctly and reduce the risk of disease. Most whole foods are lower in saturated fat, sugar and salt, the three nutrients associated with non-communicable diseases. Eating a balanced diet of whole foods, such as the Mediterranean style of eating, will be better for your health, and this has been proven many times.

As a nutritionist, I am particularly interested in the health benefits of fibre in the diet, significantly to help protect against heart disease and colorectal cancer. Despite having myriad health benefits, most of us eat very little of it. Fibre is one of the nutrients frequently highlighted as being particularly low in the typical Western diet, and the amount of fibre has been shown to drop significantly the more ultra-processed food someone eats.

Many whole foods are naturally satiating, containing more fibre and less added sugar. One of the reasons ultra-processed foods are so bad for us is that the combination of fats, sugar, salt and additives can make us want to eat more of them, contributing to weight gain.

It also should not be forgotten that whole foods often have more complex and natural flavours that can help to make the food you cook taste exquisitely superior. Just think about the many different herbs and spices available to us. Ultra-processed food tastes addictively good because food manufacturers spend a lot of time and money trying to artificially recreate and enhance the flavours commonly found in nature.

I have mentioned several times that researchers suspect that the additives in ultra-processed foods are causing us harm. Prioritizing whole foods is the simplest way to ensure that what you're eating is free of these industrially used compounds. As you reduce your intake of UPF your palate changes and you become less reliant on salt and sugar. These adaptations in taste preference can increase your enjoyment of the flavours found naturally in fresh whole foods.

Get to grips with the food label and unprocessed or minimally processed foods

Suppose you are going to live an unprocessed life. In that case, you need to understand how to interpret the information given to you on the food label. There is plenty of information on pages 22–26 to help you identify ultra-processed food and decide what to choose from when you must buy something out of the home. The degree of processing can vary between similar food products, so reading the label can help you find trusted brands that produce minimally processed foods you can include in your unprocessed life.

It is not impossible to find something unprocessed from the high street that you can eat 'on the go', but it is also not easy. Understanding what foods are available to you can help you to cobble something together from your favourite high-street food outlet, even if that is just a chicken breast, bag of salad, nuts, seeds and a squeeze of lemon juice and olive oil. You can find examples of which foods fall into each NOVA category on pages 12–16.

Discover a passion for cooking

You can't live an unprocessed life without doing some cooking, and one of the reasons you have decided to read this book is to get some food inspiration. There is something for everyone in this book, so if you are new to cooking, then start simple and choose recipes that are easy to follow. I recommend the traybake, skewer and pie recipes as an excellent place to kick off.

You will only improve your interest, confidence and skills in the kitchen if you cook regularly, even if this is just once a week to batch-cook a few dishes. It's good to go off plan sometimes to experiment with new flavours or adapt some of the recipes in this book by adding fresh herbs and spices (the basic tomato sauce and versatile red pepper sauce are perfect for this). Once you have learnt the basics of living an unprocessed life, explore other cookbooks and websites for new and exciting dishes that may use a particular cuisine you have enjoyed cooking.

Cooking with others can also help you get inspired, whether with friends over a glass of wine or with your kids, as you help educate them about eating healthily. I also recommend getting the right kitchen kit to make the whole experience more enjoyable. Suppose anything will turn you off from cooking. In that case, it is trying to cut vegetables with a blunt knife, food sticking to the bottom of a pan, or needing the right-sized bowl to mix your ingredients. Later in this book, you will find a section on the recommended equipment to kit your kitchen out with.

It would help if you viewed the health benefits of living an unprocessed life as a driver to changing how you eat and cooking your food from scratch.

Make time for food

One of the main reasons we succumb to ultra-processed food is convenience, which means we should be making time for food. Suppose you want to live an unprocessed life. In that case, you need to develop a good relationship with food, which means dedicating time to think about, prepare and eat it. If you don't set time aside to eat or are a regular meal skipper, you are more likely to opt for ultra-processed snack foods and quick-fix meals. From a nutrition and health perspective, making time for food means you may be more likely to make healthier food choices.

In contrast, the time you dedicate can be used to prepare and enjoy nourishing meals. This nourishment will help support your good health, physical performance and mental alertness. These factors can all be compromised when you live on a diet of ultra-processed foods that lack essential nutrients, promote weight gain, encourage poor digestion, and can play havoc with your blood sugar levels.

Making time for food can also support your emotional well-being as you share meals in social surroundings with family and friends. Eating mindfully by savouring the meal you spent the time to cook can help you to develop a better relationship with food and turn eating into a calming and stress-reducing activity, giving you time to relax, even in the middle of a busy day.

Whilst making time for food is essential, if you start cooking from scratch and preparing food in advance, it is part of a bigger picture of self-care. Recognizing the vital role of food and nourishment can positively impact your health and overall well-being.

Overcoming the challenges of living an unprocessed life

_____

Your journey to living an unprocessed life may present some challenges when lifestyle gets in the way. There is no timeline to this journey, and it may be something you dip in and out of for a while or dedicate yourself to completely. Still, either way, if you put the love in, it will love you back concerning your health. The first few weeks will be the most engaging and challenging as you adjust to dedicating more focus to eating differently. There are plenty of things to think about to help you reduce your intake of ultra-processed foods.

Plan ahead
————

Suppose you think about what you will eat across the week and what you need to achieve this. In that case, you are less likely to lose the motivation to live an unprocessed life, and achieve your desired outcome. Approaching your journey in an organized and structured way involves meal planning, shopping and batch-cooking, which I have touched upon several times already and explained how to do this. Planning this way can also help you manage your food bill more efficiently and reduce the amount of wasted food in your kitchen.

Planning will also help remove the stress and anxiety from mealtimes, which is another reason why people often turn to convenience foods, especially when feeding their kids or after a very hectic day at work. If you know what you will be eating across the week, then this can also lessen the chance of you and anyone else you are cooking for making impulsive and unhealthy food choices, and ensure all mealtimes are free of ultra-processed foods.

Learn to batch-cook and freeze your food

I have mentioned this already... several times. Still, batch-cooking and freezing your food is something to get to grips with if you want to save time and cook from scratch only a few times a week. A lack of time is one of the main reasons clients tell me they cannot cook something healthy for themselves. I don't really agree with this as I believe you should make time for food, and it is more about shifting your focus and adapting your lifestyle to accommodate mealtimes. This is more about having a lack of interest in food or a passion for cooking, which can be worked on. If you batch-cook and freeze your food, you may only have to cook once or twice a week, and we all have time for that.

Start slowly

Stay calm, as living an unprocessed life can be an adjustment to your lifestyle and take a little time. It's easy to get overwhelmed, which I experienced myself when testing the recipes for this book and trying to make dozens of sauces and dressings at once. Start with the most used items in your cupboard, like condiments, breads, stocks and granola. You want to get to the point where it becomes second nature to batch-cook these simple everyday food items so you always have them in stock.

Flick through the recipe pages of this book and find a repertoire of simple recipes you can easily manage within the constraints of your lifestyle but also the dishes that appeal to you the most so you feel inspired to cook them. You may commonly buy plenty of unprocessed versions of ultra-processed

foods, including chicken Kyivs, melt-in-the-middle fishcakes, Vietnamese pho, pot noodles or meat pies. Let your curiosity lead as you discover how to make these dishes yourself. Become proficient in quickly whipping these meals up and cooking double quantities to keep a stock in the fridge or freezer for later in the week or months ahead.

Educate yourself about ultra-processed foods

If you are keen to live an unprocessed life, then read up on the subject. Authors such as Chris van Tulleken (Ultra Processed People) have brought the conversation to the forefront and explained the topic in a current, scientifically sound way, and delivered simply and in the relevant context to help you understand what it is all about.

Reading around the topic can offer valuable insight and knowledge that can empower you to make informed food choices, stick to your goal of embracing the unprocessed life and reduce your intake of ultra-processed foods. Understanding an ultra-processed diet's potential adverse health outcomes can be a powerful incentive to remain steadfast in your goals of living an unprocessed life.

Exploring healthier alternatives is what this book is all about, and understanding more about ultra-processed foods will make this book even more relevant to your new way of thinking. This will incentivise you to reduce your intake of ultra-processed foods by cooking from scratch at home and sharing your newfound passion for unprocessed eating with those around you.

Get friends and family on board

Take what you have learnt about ultra-processed foods and use this knowledge to educate others and inspire them to make their own unprocessed life journey. As a family, it can be a shared journey to get the whole family to develop healthier eating habits. Even your family's most avid meat eaters could surprise you with a newfound enjoyment of vegetarian or vegan dishes. You can also host diners at your home to cook for friends to show how easy it can be to produce versions of commonly eaten ultra-processed foods.

There is a section in the book about feeding the kids. All these recipes can be prepared by you and your children, so use this to help them understand how food is made and where it comes from.

Choose foods to suit your lifestyle

To make living an unprocessed life work for you, you must find dishes you want to eat. This book is not about dieting, detoxing or eliminating food groups from your diet but embracing eating whole foods and cooking from scratch to improve your health.

It doesn't matter if you eat the same things several times a week, to begin with, as you find your feet through the recipe section of the book and figure out how to fit mealtimes around your lifestyle.

I make Tortilla pizza (see page 128) several times weekly for my lunch and add different toppings, because I can whip them up in 5 minutes flat using homemade Wholemeal tortilla (see page 190) I have batch-cooked at the start of the week. I also

have a regular supply of single-portion batches of frozen Chicken tikka masala (see page 84), Middle Eastern aubergine and lentil stew (see page 114) and Coconut dahl with roasted beetroot (see page 120) that I regularly take with me when I work in the office. If I know I am working away from home during the week, I will also batch-cook snacks such as the High-protein energy bars (see page 177) I can take with me. I even keep a bag of homemade Pecan and coconut granola (see page 74) with me sometimes, to nibble on when I get hungry running between meetings.

Your lifestyle is personal to you, and only you know the time you have and when you can eat, so factor this in when planning what to eat across the week.

Develop healthy eating patterns

I don't have a problem with snacking. In fact, my very active lifestyle means I include several snacks/small meals daily between breakfast, lunch and dinner. It is more of an issue when there is no need for extra energy across the day or you are eating out of boredom or seeking comfort. These are moments when we often turn to the ultra-processed snacks that make it into our weekly shopping baskets. Even the so-called 'healthy' snacks like granola bars, protein bars and savoury crackers are laden with ultra-processed additives.

The purpose of this book is not to tell you when or what you should be eating, as this is your choice. However, developing a healthy eating pattern can help lessen your opportunities to eat something ultra-processed. Focusing on unprocessed whole foods is a good way to promote satiety and relieve the urge to snack between meals.

Commonly asked questions

On my journey to living an unprocessed life, I have been asked many questions by friends and family and have read plenty of articles and magazine features where other queries and confusion has cropped up. This section will answer some of those questions to satisfy your curiosity and smooth the way to eating less ultra-processed foods.

Can you drink alcohol?

There are no health benefits to drinking alcohol, and you should stick to the recommended advice on this. As far as drinking alcohol when living an unprocessed life, it's about knowing which drinks to choose. Alcohol can differ significantly in production methods, additives and processing techniques. Wine, beer and cider would be considered processed but only ultra-processed for sugary fruit-flavoured versions, especially cider. Spirits, both white and brown, are considered ultra-processed by the NOVA system because they have undergone a process of distillation after fermentation, which includes various additives. Some whiskies have food colouring added to them (E150a – caramel colouring).

Do you have to avoid ultra-processed foods all the time?

How you approach living an unprocessed life is up to you. Still, I recommend reducing your intake of these foods, which you can continue to decrease over time. This approach is more likely to get longer-lasting results. Many of the fond food memories we share with friends revolve around certain foods, and many of these are ultra-processed. I feel very passionately about people adopting specific diets in an extreme way only to give them up shortly afterwards and move on to the next diet trend. Again, it goes back to being realistic to get long-lasting results – will you turn down a fancy cocktail with your mates or birthday cake with your child forever? Probably not, so take the view that these are once-in-a-while foods, but most of the time, you live unprocessed.

What about eating out?

Eating out of the home can be challenging when trying to live an unprocessed life. This book has a section on packed lunches that you can take to work with you, and of course, you can also use leftovers. Not all food that is produced out of the home is ultra-processed. There are healthy options in many high-street food outlets, like salads and grain-based dishes. However, you should still check the label to see what is in it. Usually, the elements like salad dressings, marinades and spice mixes contain additives.

You can buy unprocessed or minimally processed ingredients to create a minimally processed lunch at work, such as a bag of salad or a pouch of ready-cooked grains with canned legumes, lean proteins (fish, poultry, tofu), lemon juice, olive oil and herbs. When eating out at restaurants, it depends on where you eat. Many high-street restaurants use manufactured sauces to create their food. In contrast, others may produce mostly freshly cooked, which you can navigate more easily.

Is it wrong to use canned food?

This depends on what is in the can. This is where some people start to need clarification with the definition of processed. Some whole foods are canned to help make them easier to use and to preserve them so you can keep them in store for longer. These are processed, but I would call them healthy processed foods, including canned legumes, fish, fruits and vegetables such as tomatoes using water or natural juices. In my recipes, I use dried legumes and primarily fresh produce. Still, you can swap these for healthy processed canned foods. Still, you must check the label for ultra-processed ingredients (this does not include salt added to canned tuna, for example).

Is it more expensive to live an unprocessed life?

Cooking from scratch will be more expensive than filling your shopping basket with cheap, ready meals. Still, it doesn't mean that living an unprocessed life is necessarily costly. There are ways to save on your food bill by choosing seasonal vegetables or frozen alternatives, which is the same for fish and seafood. You can also buy cheaper cuts of meat, such as the thigh or a whole chicken, and use it throughout the week. In dishes that use meat, you can replace half with beans, pulses and lentils, which are very cheap when you buy them dry and soak them yourself. It's also essential to save on food waste by choosing recipes that use the foods you have left in the fridge, freezer or food cupboard.

Can you eat white carbs?

Foods such as white pasta, couscous and rice are minimally processed foods with health benefits. My recipes use wholemeal and wholegrain varieties of foods simply because they are less processed and have added health benefits in fibre and mineral content. It is absolutely fine for you to switch wholemeal and wholegrain varieties of foods for their white counterparts if that makes meals more palatable for you.

What if I have no time to make a sauce, dressing or bread?

Making these foods from scratch does take time, and time is only sometimes on our side when life goes into overdrive. This is why people are drawn to convenient ultra-processed foods in the first place. The best solution here is to get to grips with making a healthier food choice by reading the labels on shop-bought foods. Some are, in fact, classed as minimally processed, and you can seek out less processed breads at your local bakery. Make time for food and batch-cook these foods, then freeze them, giving you plenty of options.

Can you still eat sugar?

You don't have to avoid sweet foods altogether when following an unprocessed diet. This way of eating is to choose whole foods in their most natural and unaltered state, so I suggest sticking to honey (maple syrup if you're vegan) and avoiding cane sugar, industrialised sweeteners and artificial sweeteners. Sweetness can also be

achieved in foods by using fruits like dates. Still, creating certain dishes without honey to sweeten them is only sometimes possible, especially the snacks and puddings in this book. You can cut all sweeteners out of your diet completely, but this refers to being realistic about what you want to do long-term. This book is intended to make living an unprocessed life simple and achievable in the long term. If avoiding all sweeteners is an approach you want to take, I suggest doing this gradually. Hence, it is a habit change that sticks and is not just another 'flash in the pan' health kick.

Do I need to buy organic food?

You should always buy the best quality food you can with the budget you have. If you choose to eat organic, this has its benefits, but it is optional when living an unprocessed life. In fact, there are plenty of ultra-processed foods labelled organic, so don't let this fool you when deciding what to eat.

Is shop-bought vegan food ultra-processed?

Food that is suitable for a vegan diet, such as canned beans, pulses and lentils, are minimally processed foods and are a valuable addition nutritionally to a healthy vegan diet. When the veganism trend exploded and became more about plant-based eating, the food industry quickly reacted by producing 'alternative' versions of common meat-based foods and plant-based ready meals and snacks. I am not saying these are all unhealthy. Still, many are ultra-processed and use thickeners, gelling agents, flavourings and colourings to achieve the right texture and taste.

Equipment

Cooking with good-quality pots, pans and knives can make a real difference in how your food turns out. Investing in a few good pieces can make preparing and cooking food a more accessible and more enjoyable experience. Here are a few suggestions for the bits of kitchen kit I can't do without, some of which you may already have.

NON-STICK DEEP-SIDED FRYING PAN

A good-quality deep-sided frying pan is worth investing in, and I cook everything in mine, from stews and stir-fries to a fried egg. Investing in non-stick is a much more enjoyable cooking experience, and it also means you use less oil, which lends itself well to a healthier way of cooking.

NON-STICK BAKING TRAYS

I have cooked at many clients' houses only to realize they need a baking tray. This doesn't sound like such a big deal until you start cooking and a recipe wants you to toast some seeds or roast a vegetable. Get a few in different sizes, as they are convenient.

MEASURING SPOONS

This is an obvious bit of kitchen equipment. Still, it is much easier to follow a recipe when you have the correct size measuring spoons instead of having to guess how much to put in. It's not the end of the world if you add a tad too much oil or dried spice, but it just feels more of an efficient way of cooking.

FOOD PROCESSOR AND BLENDER

I use a medium-sized food processor (Magimix) often when cooking and have done so for many recipes in this book. This food processor has a smaller fitting, which helps make pastes. You can invest in a high-powered blender like a Nutribullet or Vitamix, which are superior when making sauces, milk and dressings, but to be honest, you can manage with a food processor.

CHEESECLOTH

You will need these when making some of the sauces and milk in this book, especially if you are using a food processor over a high-powered blender. You can also use nut milk bags or muslin cloth if that is easier to find. You can typically find these in a kitchen store or order online.

GLASS JARS AND BOTTLES

Glassware is a lovely way to store your sauces, dressings, granola, and other such dishes you use daily. Try using nice Kilner jars and bottles with a good airtight sealable top. Remember a funnel, which sounds obvious until you are caught short trying to decant a vat of ketchup into a glass bottle, which, without one, is not easy to navigate.

AIRTIGHT CONTAINERS FOR FREEZING

Get plenty of these if you intend on freezing your food. Good-quality reusable plastic containers are a better choice than the ones you can only use once. Glass containers can also be used to freeze food but not liquids, as they are prone to smashing as the liquid expands. Get a variety of sizes for different batch sizes.

JULIENNE PEELER

I love these peelers, and they are a different way to prepare your vegetables for salads, and the only way to make courgetti, which is featured in this book. You can buy them in kitchen shops and online.

How to freeze food

_____

Understanding how to freeze food is a non-negotiable when living an unprocessed life. Not only does freezing food properly help to prolong its life, but it also helps to protect the quality, texture and taste, keeping it palatable and tasting at its best when you defrost and reheat it again. As everything in this book is cooked from scratch, cooking in batches and freezing your food is easier and more cost-effective. Most of the recipes in this book have individual advice on how to freeze. There are also many ways to help avoid food waste by freezing leftover foods such as herbs and vegetables.

Start with good quality ingredients

The quality of your food will not improve with freezing. Prepare your meals with the best quality ingredients within the limits of access and budget you have for food.

Get the temperature down quickly

Make sure all hot food has completely cooled down before you freeze it. You can speed up the cooling process by splitting the batches into smaller containers. This is often a better way of freezing, so you have meals available to serve one or two people.

Pick a suitable container

Choose a suitable container to freeze your dish. Rigid airtight containers made from plastic or glass are ideal for solid food, as are Ziplock bags. These containers will prevent freezer burn and moisture loss or strong odours from affecting the food. Avoid glass for freezing liquids, as they can cause cracking when the liquid expands.

Label and date your food

Clearly labelling your food with the name and date it 'expires' is essential. I have often found containers and had no idea what was in them or when I cooked them. Organizing your freezer is really satisfying, especially after a batch-cooking session.

Freeze your food quickly

Freezing your food quickly can help to improve its flavour and texture. Store your newly packaged food in the coldest part of your freezer, usually the rear centre. Make sure that your freezer temperature is set to -18°C or lower.

Keep your food airtight

Always use airtight, sealable containers; if you are using bags, try to remove as much air from them as possible before freezing. Packaging your food this way will help to prevent freezer burn.

Freezer times

Most foods can be stored safely for several months, but they are best used within 3-6 months to preserve their quality.

Thaw and cook thoroughly

When you are ready to use your dish then defrost it in the fridge or use the defrost setting on a microwave. Thawing at room temperature can encourage bacterial growth. When the food is ready to cook then make sure it is cooked thoroughly and piping hot before serving.

Food	Freezer time	Tips
Pastes such as pesto and curry	6 months	Try freezing in ice-cube trays then pop out and store in a Ziplock bag.
Stock	6 months	Try freezing in ice-cube trays then pop out and store in a Ziplock bag.
Milk and nut milks	3-6 months	
Blanched or par-cooked vegetables	1 year	
Fruit	1 year	Chop before freezing and remove hard peels like banana or avocado skins.
Cooked meat dishes	3 months	Freeze in smaller batches for convenience.
Cooked legumes, grains or dishes that use them	3 months	Freeze in smaller batches for convenience.
Cooked rice	3 months	Leave to cool completely then place in a sealable bag, remove as much air as possible and label. You can microwave from frozen.
Cooked fish dishes	3 months	Freeze in smaller batches for convenience.
Cakes and sweet breads	3 months	You may want to slice before freezing or divide into smaller pieces before freezing.
Bread (loaf, pitta, tortilla, breadcrumbs)	3 months	Slice before freezing to save waste and defrost in the toaster.

How to batch-cook

____

One of the main reasons we eat ultra-processed foods is because they are convenient. Batch-cooking is a way to create your own convenience, and by dedicating a specific day or certain days to cooking, you can free up precious time during the rest of the week. Knowing you have something healthy to eat when you don't feel like cooking is a real gem when you get used to preparing food this way.

Bulk buying ingredients is also a cost-effective way to purchase your food, and having something in store can often help reduce the temptation of ordering takeaways or eating out, especially when trying to reduce your food bill. When you batch-cook food, you also save on food waste and energy bills as you can plan and use leftover foods in your fridge or cupboard.

Before you start, get organized. Batch-cooking seems simple. Double up the recipe quantity, portion it into containers, and then put it in the fridge or freezer. This is great, but if you want to get the most out of your batch-cooking, you may need to put more thought into it.

My previous experience of batch-cooking is a lesson learnt. I would cook a giant vat of something (usually just one dish) and then freeze it. However, the thrill of having Quorn Bolognese on tap quickly wore thin. I also realized that the cheap containers I bought were not microwavable, so my healthy convenience food needed to be defrosted before cooking, and often, I would eat something else and throw the Quorn Bolognese away. The containers were also meant to be reusable, but they cracked when I had pried the tops off. I also noticed that some tubs had freezer burn as the lids weren't airtight, which ruined the quality of my glorious Quorn Bolognese. Also, it's a great idea to label your food. How many of us have found a random plastic pot glued with ice to the back of our freezers and had no idea what was in it until we managed to get the top off of it.

To avoid my experience of batch-cooking, start by keeping a list of the recipes you will be cooking from this book, and you can also look for recipes that help you use leftover foods. Note the ones that work well in batches, as some will be better than others. Make sure you have a good variety of foods so you can enjoy what you have cooked, and you can also explore other ways of serving your batch-cooked meals. For example, a beef chilli can be served with rice, wrapped in a flour tortilla with salad or used to top a jacket potato.

Invest in high-quality containers as this will help to preserve your food and give you nice ways of serving your food, like glass bottles for ketchup and nut milk, or Mason and Kilner jars for mayonnaise. It is also a good idea to work out how you will portion your food as it may be more convenient to freeze or refrigerate it in single serving sizes if you plan to take it to work with you, or bigger servings depending on the size of your family. Here are my simple steps to batch-cooking...

Plan your meals

This will help you understand what meal occasions you are planning food for and the number of days you want the food to last in the fridge or freezer.

Pick your recipes

Some recipes work better than others for keeping in the fridge or freezing, so I would recommend one-pot dishes (soups, stews, casseroles and baked dishes), grain bowls and salads, flavoured proteins (fish, chicken, tofu), granola, frittatas and home-bakes (brownies or energy bars). You can also batch-cook bread products or even sauces for future use.

Some recipes work better than others when scaled up to batch-cook, so consider this. Baked goods like cakes, frittatas and bread are unlikely to work in a bigger size, so always stick to the recipe and cook two rather than one bigger version. Recipes with a lot of sauce can often become too 'saucy' when scaled up. It won't reduce as much in the time it takes to cook the dish, so reduce the extra liquid to only half or three-quarters of the original recipe.

Jot down your shopping list

Get everything ready before you start cooking, as there is nothing more annoying than going to all this effort to find you are missing a vital ingredient once you have already begun to do so. Keep your cupboards and fridge organized and check what you already have in stock to avoid unnecessary spending and food waste.

Get your containers ready

Have all this organized before you start cooking, and know which dish is going in what container based on the portion size. You also need to check what containers are suitable for freezing as you cannot put liquids into glass bottles, for instance. Check what containers can be used to reheat your food if you are doing so in a microwave or oven.

Cooking equipment

Make sure you have the right-sized bowls, pots, pans and roasting trays to accommodate the larger sizes of the food you are preparing.

Cooking process

Work through the recipes and find what you can cook or prepare in bulk before cooking. This might be a large batch of different grains or a pile of chopped onions, garlic or red peppers used in multiple recipes.

Label and store

Once you have portioned your food into the suitable containers, label them with the dish's name and the date you prepared it. Think about when you are most likely to eat your prepared food. There is no point in putting it in the freezer if you eat it a few days later as it will store perfectly well in the fridge rather than waiting to defrost it.

Unprocessed pantry

On your journey to living an unprocessed life, you may find you regularly use the same type of foods. Throughout this cookbook, some store cupboard essentials feature in many recipes, so consider stocking up on them as part of planning and organizing yourself in the kitchen.

Legumes

This group of foods include beans, lentils and peas. If you are using dried legumes, except for lentils and mung beans, they must be soaked overnight before you can use them. Soaking helps to remove harmful substances such as lectins, which are exceptionally high in red kidney beans. The process of soaking also helps to improve the digestibility of legumes (reducing levels of oligosaccharides that can cause bloating and gas), deactivate anti-nutrients such as phytates and tannins, which can interfere with the absorption of certain minerals, and reduce the cooking time.

In this cookbook, the legumes in recipes are given as prepared, so you can use dried versions you have soaked and cooked, or canned. Canned legumes are classed as a minimally processed food, which means they have been made more convenient to consume but not in a way that is bad for your health.

The conversion for dried legumes to canned is 100g to 400g can (contains 240g of soaked and cooked legumes). As a rule of thumb, raw legumes double in size once they have been soaked and cooked.

HOW TO PREPARE DRIED LEGUMES

1. Tip the legumes into a sieve or colander and re-move any that are damaged or discoloured, small stones or debris that has found its way into the packet. Now rinse the beans under cold water.
2. Soak your legumes overnight for 8-12 hours. Transfer the rinsed legumes to a large bowl and cover them with plenty of cold water, as they will expand to double the size on average.
3. Drain the legumes in a sieve or colander, then transfer to a saucepan and cover with fresh water about 5cm above them. You might want to add salt, pepper and fresh herbs, such as a bay leaf or thyme, but it's not essential. Bring the water to the boil, then reduce the heat and simmer until they are tender and easily mash between your fingers. This varies depending on the legume but could take up to 1.5 hours.
4. Once cooked, you can drain your legumes and cool them completely. You can use them immediately or store them for 3-4 days in an airtight container in the fridge. You can also store cooked legumes in the freezer for up to 6 months, so if you use them regularly, it may be worth batch-cooking them. Remember to freeze them in suitable portion sizes for convenience.

Wholegrains

Wholegrains are unprocessed starchy foods, including wheat, rye, barley, oats and rice. The fact they are unprocessed means they retain their fibre-rich outer layer, which is removed on white versions of these grains. Good wholegrains to keep in stock are short-grain brown rice, wholemeal pasta, wholemeal couscous, pearl barley and oats. Quinoa can be included here even though it is a seed or what is commonly referred to as a pseudo-grain.

Nuts and seeds

These foods are valuable ingredients to make healthy, unprocessed snack foods and as toppers for salads or to eat alone as a snack. Nuts and seeds offer a good source of protein, omega-3 and nutrients such as magnesium, iron and B vitamins. Use raw, unsalted varieties, which you can toast for more flavour. To save on cost, buy nuts and seeds in bulk online or seek out multipack offers from your local health food store. Homemade nut butter is used in several recipes. You can use shop-bought as long as it is minimally processed (see page 22).

Oils

Extra virgin olive oil is the purest of unrefined oils. It is obtained from the first pressing with the least amount of processing. Cold-pressed varieties tell us that the oil has been extracted using no heat, which helps retain more nutritional benefits. Refined oils are processed using chemicals that remove nutrients, enzymes and other compounds, which makes them more tolerant to higher heat. The smoking point for extra virgin olive oil is 160°C–190°C, which makes it suitable for most home cooking. Some extra virgin olive oils have a more intense flavour, which you may want to reserve for drizzling over food. Sometimes, recipes use non-virgin olive oil because the taste can be overpowering.

Honey

Let's begin by saying all sweeteners in any form are still sugar. I have used minimal sugar in these recipes. Still, some need more sweetening than others, such as those found in the snacks and puddings section. I have used honey throughout the book instead of refined sugar as it is closest; we have a minimally processed sweetener as it's filtered and, in some cases, pasteurized. A great tip from Nigella is to rub your spoon with oil before using the honey, which slides right off.

Flours

Wholegrain flours are ground from whole, unprocessed wheat kernels, grains and seeds. In contrast, refined flours such as white are made by processing wholegrains to remove the wheat germ and bran before milling. Throughout this book, I use wholemeal and spelt flour to make bread and thicken sauces. One or two recipes use a small amount of white all-purpose flour to help produce a lighter result.

Canned and frozen vegetables

These foods are both time- and cost-savers, but some are classed as being processed, albeit healthy and not harmful to your health. Frozen vegetables fall into the unprocessed or minimally processed food category. Keep peas, sweetcorn and mixed vegetables in your store cupboard essentials. I keep canned tomatoes, tomato purée and sweetcorn in stock, which are processed but in a way that is not bad for your health. I would always choose canned vegetables with no added salt or sugar.

Processed culinary ingredients

These are ingredients made from unprocessed foods through simple processing; you need them to create the flavour in dishes. The ingredients in this book include butter, salt, dried herbs and spices, miso, tamari sauce and vinegar.

Dried herbs and spices

It's good to keep a stock of spices you will use regularly rather than end up with dusty, out-of-date packets in the back of your food cupboard. Dried herbs and spices are minimally processed. I suggest starting with ground cumin, ground coriander, oregano, mixed herbs, smoked paprika, curry powder and dried chillies.

Breakfast

Homemade hash browns with poached egg and hot sauce

Whether you buy your browns from McDonald's or the freezer section of your local supermarket, it is hard to find one that doesn't contain ingredients you don't recognize, like dextrose. These homemade hash browns are easy to make and, topped with an egg, make a nutritious start to the day. You can also make your own Hot sauce (see page 209) instead of shop-bought sriracha to drizzle over the egg.

SERVES 4
(MAKES 8 HASH BROWNS)

4 large Maris Piper potatoes , peeled
1 onion, halved
5 large eggs, 1 beaten
1 tbsp extra virgin olive oil
Sea salt and black pepper
Hot sauce (see page 209)

- Try serving this with a dollop of homemade guacamole (see page 131), which is super tasty.
- You can batch-cook the grated potato in this recipe then freeze it to save you time when you make these later. Flash-freeze the grated potato by spreading it out on parchment paper and freezing for 1 hour uncovered. Transfer to a freezer bag or sealable container and store for up to 3 months. To use, defrost the potato for 1 hour then continue with the recipe from step 3 above.

1_ Set a deep-sided saucepan of water to boil over a medium heat.

2_ Coarsely grate the potatoes and onion onto a clean tea towel then pull all four corners together and twist over the sink to squeeze out the excess liquid.

3_ Tip the vegetables into a large bowl along with the beaten egg. Season with salt and pepper then mix well.

4_ Heat the oil in a large non-stick frying pan set over a medium-high heat. Once the oil is hot, add spoonfuls of the mixture to the pan and flatten into patties about 1cm thick. Cook for 2–3 minutes until browned, then flip and repeat on the other side.

5_ Once cooked transfer the patties to a plate and wrap in foil to keep warm.

6_ This is when the eggs need to be poached. Keep the water at a very gentle simmer and gently crack the eggs into the water. Cook for 3–4 minutes, or until the egg white has set. Gently transfer the eggs from the pan to a plate using a slotted spoon.

7_ Serve 2 hash browns on top of one another and top with an egg. Sprinkle a few drops of hot sauce over the egg before serving.

Homemade baked beans

Everyone has their favourite brand of baked beans, and the homemade variety will probably not suit everyone's taste, but they make a great alternative to tinned versions. Some brands contain glucose-fructose syrup and modified maize starch to sweeten and thicken the sauce, which makes them ultra-processed. The cannellini beans used in this recipe have the same texture as the baked beans you buy in the tin, and they are lower in sugar and salt.

SERVES 4

1 tbsp extra virgin olive oil

2 onions, sliced

2 garlic cloves, crushed

1 tbsp smoked paprika

200g dried cannellini beans, soaked and cooked (see page 64)

2 x 400g tins chopped tomatoes

1 tbsp honey

2 tbsp tamari

Toast, to serve

1_ Set a saucepan over a low-medium heat and add the oil. Once hot, add the onions and gently fry for 10 minutes until they begin to caramelize.

2_ Add the garlic and paprika and cook for 30 seconds.

3_ Turn the heat up to medium and stir in the beans, tomatoes, honey and tamari. Gently simmer for 10 minutes, stirring regularly, until the sauce has thickened.

4_ Serve straight away on toast.

- If baked beans are a regular in your house, then batch-cook a double quantity of these and store in an airtight container in the fridge to use throughout the week.
- You can also use 2 x 400g tins of cannellini beans (rinsed and drained) in place of dried in this recipe.

Sliced red peppers and cherry tomatoes on toast with chilli fried egg

This red pepper and cherry tomato sauce is an excellent base for a fried egg; when I say fried, I mean cooked in a non-stick pan with the smallest amount of oil. Red pepper and cherry tomatoes are a perfect combination of flavours, especially when the egg yolk runs over them. Try this with a good drizzle of the homemade Hot sauce (see page 209) to give your breakfast a chilli kick.

SERVES 2

1 tbsp extra virgin olive oil
1 small onion, thinly sliced
1 garlic clove, finely chopped
1 large red pepper, sliced
8 cherry tomatoes, halved
2 eggs
2 slices of bread, such as Seeded wholemeal and rye loaf (see page 191), toasted
Chilli flakes or Hot sauce (see page 209)
Sea salt and black pepper

1_ Heat the oil in a non-stick frying pan set over a medium heat.
2_ Add the onion to the pan and gently fry for 3 minutes until softened. Add the garlic, pepper and tomatoes and cook for a further 5 minutes until softened. Season with salt and pepper then take off the heat and set aside.
3_ Set another non-stick frying pan over a medium heat. Add a little oil and then crack the eggs into the pan and fry to your liking. At the same time put the bread in the toaster.
4_ Once the eggs are cooked, start to build you dish. Place the pepper mixture on top of the toast slices then add an egg on top of each and sprinkle with dried chilli flakes or a small drizzle of hot sauce.

• This dish also works well with poached eggs.

Soft-boiled eggs with Tenderstem soldiers

Sometimes the simplest dishes can be the tastiest, and nothing could be simpler than this breakfast. Eggs are a source of nearly every nutrient you need for good health, and I don't need to tell you how healthy green vegetables are! This is an excellent alternative to using packaged white bread, which is an ultra-processed food.

SERVES 2

4 large eggs, at room temperature
200g Tenderstem broccoli
Pinch of smoked paprika or
    cayenne pepper

1_ Set a large saucepan of water over a high heat and bring to the boil.

2_ Place the eggs in the pan and boil for 5–6 minutes for a runny yolk.

3_ When the eggs are almost ready throw the Tenderstem into the pan and blanch for 30 seconds, then remove with a pair of tongs and set aside on a plate.

4_ Transfer the cooked eggs from the pan to egg cups. Slice the top off the egg and sprinkle with smoked paprika or cayenne pepper.

5_ Serve with the Tenderstem dippers.

- You can also use thick asparagus here, which is in season during May and June. Snap off the woody ends and blanch for the same amount of time (slightly longer if your asparagus is very thick) to keep it nice and crunchy.

Pecan and coconut granola

While it may seem healthy, shop-bought granola is often loaded with sugar.
It does differ between brands, but many contain preservatives such as sulphur
dioxide and glucose-fructose syrup for sweetness. It's easy to make your own
from unprocessed wholegrains, nuts, nut butter, seeds and spices. Strictly
speaking this granola should have no added sugar to be classed as unprocessed,
so adding a little honey is optional.

SERVES 8

350g whole rolled oats
120g pecan nuts, chopped
60g coconut flakes
1 tbsp ground cinnamon
½ tsp sea salt
2 tbsp extra virgin olive oil
2 tbsp honey (optional)
4 tbsp Smooth almond butter (see
    page 205)

1_   Preheat the oven to 150°C/130°C fan/Gas 2 and line a
     baking sheet with parchment paper.

2_   Place all the dry ingredients in a bowl and combine. Drizzle
     in the olive oil, honey (if using) and almond butter and stir
     with a spatula until fully combined.

3_   Transfer the granola to the baking sheet and press the
     mixture into a large oval shape about 2.5cm deep with
     your hands.

4_   Bake in the oven for 15 minutes, then remove from the
     oven, rotate the baking sheet and gently break the granola
     apart slightly with a fork. Continue to bake for a further
     15 minutes until the oats are golden brown.

5_   Remove the granola from the oven and leave to cool. Once
     cool you can transfer it to an airtight container and store
     for up to 2 weeks.

•   You can freeze homemade granola
    in an airtight container or vacuum
    pack (with as little air space as
    possible) for up to 3 months. To
    defrost just leave it overnight on
    your kitchen worktop.

Soaked oats with pomegranate and coconut

This is a delicious unprocessed breakfast that ticks many nutritional boxes. Oats are high in fibre, which is good for your heart, while milk is a source of calcium (good for your bones) and B12, which helps you to convert food into energy and make healthy red blood cells. You can add many different toppings to this basic recipe, including fruits, nuts, nut butter, seeds and spices.

SERVES 2

100g porridge oats
200ml apple juice, preferably
    freshly juiced
75ml skimmed milk (or dairy-
    free alternative)
Pinch of ground cinnamon
Zest and juice of ½ lime
1 tsp honey
1 apple, grated
2 tbsp pomegranate seeds
2 tbsp coconut shavings

1_ Place the oats in a large bowl and cover with the apple juice, milk, cinnamon, lime zest and juice and honey. Combine and cover with cling film, then place in the fridge and leave to soak for 25 minutes.
2_ Remove from the fridge and stir through the grated apple.
3_ Spoon into bowls and top with pomegranate seeds and coconut shavings.

- You can top these soaked oats with anything you like such as chopped fruit, dried fruit, nuts, seeds, or Smooth nut butter (see page 205).

Breakfast

Chocolate and banana natural protein shake

Protein shakes can contain many ingredients that classify them as an ultra-processed food, including soy lecithin (which is used as an emulsifier), thickeners and artificial sweeteners such as sucralose. While they may be less convenient, homemade shakes are more nutritious and unprocessed. This shake offers you around 20g of protein, which is recommended to support muscle repair and growth post-training.

SERVES 1

250ml skimmed milk (or dairy-
    free alternative)
1 small banana, peeled and sliced
125g natural low-fat yoghurt
1 tbsp cocoa powder (unsweetened)
1 tbsp Smooth almond butter (see
    page 205)
Honey, to taste

1_   Place all the ingredients in a blender with a few cubes of ice and blitz until smooth.

• If you are trying to gain weight, then add ½ avocado and swap the skimmed milk and low-fat yoghurt for full-fat varieties.

Everyday Meals

Thai green king prawn curry

This fragrant curry has a vital essence of lime, and making your own paste makes all the difference to the flavour. Don't be put off by the long list of ingredients, as they all get thrown in a food processor to create the paste. You can also make the paste in batches to keep in the fridge or freeze. The curry is lighter when using homemade coconut milk, but it is thickened with sweet, sliced onions.

SERVES 4

1 tbsp extra virgin olive oil
2 onions, thinly sliced
4 tbsp Thai green curry paste (see below)
1 small head of broccoli, cut into small
    florets
400ml Coconut milk (see page 203)
2 pak choi, sliced lengthways
300g raw king prawns (defrosted if
    frozen), peeled
2 tbsp tamari
Zest and juice of ½ lime
Handful of coriander leaves, chopped

FOR THE PASTE

1 lemongrass stalk, outer leaves
    removed and finely chopped
4 green chillies
3 garlic cloves
1 tsp ground coriander
2.5cm piece of galangal, peeled and
    chopped
3 shallots, peeled and chopped
4 lime leaves, thinly sliced (use the zest
    of 1 lime if you can't find them)
Handful of coriander, leaves and stalks,
    chopped
Juice of 1 lime
1 tbsp tamari
2 tbsp olive oil

1_ Make the paste by adding all the ingredients to a small food processor and blitzing until smooth. Add a little more oil to help combine if it needs it. Transfer the paste to a sealable jar and keep in the fridge until needed.

2_ Set a large, deep-sided non-stick frying pan or wok over a medium heat and add the oil. Once hot, add the onions and cook for 5 minutes to soften. If they start to brown, then turn the heat down a little. Stir in the Thai green curry paste and fry for 30 seconds.

3_ Add the broccoli florets to the pan and cook for a further 30 seconds to coat in the paste.

4_ Pour in the coconut milk and bring the curry to a gentle simmer. Add the pak choi, prawns, tamari, lime zest and juice and cook for 5 minutes. It will look a little full in the pan, but the vegetables will wilt when you start to move them around. Once cooked, stir in the coriander and take off the heat.

5_ Serve with brown rice.

- Leftover paste can be kept in the fridge for a week. You can make it in a larger batch and freeze for up to 3 months. You can also freeze the curry for up to 3 months.
- If you are using a tin of coconut milk, then look for a brand that is just coconut and water (such as Biona) as many brands contain emulsifiers and stabilizers.
- If your coconut milk has been in the fridge, then give it a shake. Don't worry if there are lumps of coconut cream as they will dissolve in the curry.

Chicken Kyiv

These are a hugely popular choice when it comes to ready meals although the quality varies considerably – some just use chopped and shaped chicken pieces. The garlic purées and flavourings used in shop-bought versions are usually overpowering and excessively salty, which you don't get when you make them yourself using whole chicken breasts filled with fresh homemade garlic butter.

SERVES 4

80g unsalted butter, at room
    temperature
2 garlic cloves
Small handful of flat-leaf parsley,
    finely chopped
4 skinless chicken breasts
4 tbsp wholemeal flour
2 eggs, beaten
120g wholemeal breadcrumbs
Extra virgin olive oil, for frying
Sea salt and black pepper

1_ Put the butter, garlic and parsley into a bowl and season with salt and pepper. Combine the ingredients together then spoon onto a piece of cling film and shape into a log about 10cm long. Place in the freezer and leave for 15 minutes.

2_ Place the chicken breasts on a piece of cling film then lay another piece on top and bash with a rolling pin until flat. Take the butter from the freezer and slice into rounds, then divide them evenly across the middle of each chicken breast. Bring the edges of the chicken over the butter to form a parcel then place seam side down on a plate and chill in the fridge for 10 minutes.

3_ Preheat the oven to 200°C/180°C fan/Gas 6.

4_ Place the flour and a pinch of salt in a bowl and combine. Prepare two more bowls – one with the beaten egg and one with the breadcrumbs. Remove the Kyivs from the fridge and season each one with a dusting of the seasoned flour, then dip in the egg and then the breadcrumbs, ensuring they are fully coated.

5_ Add a few glugs of oil to a large non-stick frying pan set over a medium-high heat. Place the Kyivs in the pan with the seal facing down and fry for 5–7 minutes, turning regularly to brown each side. Transfer the Kyivs to a baking tray and bake in the oven for 12–15 minutes until golden brown and cooked through.

6_ Serve with mashed potato and green vegetables.

• You can freeze chicken Kyivs for up to 3 months. Freeze them on a baking sheet and when firm either wrap them in cling film or transfer to an airtight container or freezer bag.

Chicken tikka masala

This is one of the nation's favourite curries ordered in restaurants and takeaways. Chicken tikka masala is also a popular ready meal, both frozen and fresh. Making your own from scratch means you can improve the nutritional content and quality of the curry. The cucumber salad is traditionally called kachumber, although this is simplified here.

SERVES 4

1 tbsp extra virgin olive oil
1 small onion, chopped
1 red pepper, thinly sliced
3 garlic cloves, chopped
2.5cm piece of fresh ginger, peeled and grated
2 tsp garam masala
1 tsp chilli powder, cayenne pepper, or dried chillies
1 tsp each ground turmeric, cumin and coriander
1 tsp sweet paprika
3 tbsp tomato purée
8 large skinless and boneless chicken thighs (about 1kg)
500g tomato passata
100ml double cream
Sea salt
Coriander leaves, to garnish

FOR THE SALAD
1 cucumber, peeled, deseeded and sliced into half-moons
1 red onion, finely diced
2 tomatoes, deseeded and diced
Handful of coriander, chopped
1 tbsp olive oil
Juice of 1 lime

1_ Heat the oil in a large deep-sided non-stick frying pan set over a medium heat. Add the onion and red pepper then cook for 5 minutes until softened.

2_ Add the garlic and ginger and cook for 1 minute. Stir in the spices (use less chilli or cayenne if you prefer less heat) and cook for 1 minute until they become fragrant, then add the tomato purée and cook for a further minute.

3_ Add the chicken thighs and stir to coat in the marinade. Cook for 3–4 minutes to seal the meat, then add the passata and 100ml water. Simmer gently for 15 minutes until the chicken is cooked through.

4_ Meanwhile, prepare the salad by adding all the ingredients to a bowl and combining well. Season with a little salt then put in the fridge until ready to serve.

5_ Take the curry off the heat and stir in the cream. Taste and season with salt and garnish with coriander leaves.

6_ Serve with brown rice, Wholemeal pitta bread (see page 194) and the cucumber salad.

- Swap the double cream for yoghurt or crème fraîche for a lighter sauce.
- You can freeze this curry for up to 3 months.

Everyday Meals

Turkey meatballs with spicy red pepper sauce

These meatballs are quick and easy to prepare and can be made in bulk and frozen for future use. A big part of living an unprocessed life is learning to be versatile with leftover food to help save you time in the kitchen. This recipe is an excellent way to use up any batches of red pepper sauce, which in this case has been bulked out with tomatoes to make the sauce go further, as well as adding spice and the smoky flavour of paprika.

SERVES 4

500g turkey mince
3 spring onions, thinly sliced
2 garlic cloves, finely chopped
2 tsp ground cumin
2 tsp ground coriander
Handful of flat-leaf parsley or
  coriander, finely chopped
1 egg, beaten
1 tbsp extra virgin olive oil
Sea salt and black pepper

FOR THE SAUCE
1 batch of Versatile roasted red pepper
  sauce (see page 200)
400g tin chopped tomatoes
1 red chilli, chopped
1 tsp smoked paprika

1_ Put the turkey mince, spring onions, garlic, spices, parsley and egg into a bowl with a good pinch of salt and pepper. Mix everything together to combine well, then roll the mixture into 20 meatballs, using wet hands to stop the meat from sticking. Place the balls on a baking tray then cover and keep in the fridge for 25 minutes.

2_ Now prepare the sauce on page 200, adding the chopped tomatoes, chilli and smoked paprika to the blender with the roasted red peppers.

3_ To cook the meatballs, set a large non-stick frying pan over a medium heat and add the oil. Once hot, add the meatballs and fry for 10 minutes, turning occasionally to cook evenly on all sides. Transfer the red pepper sauce to the frying pan and cook for a further 10 minutes until the meatballs are completely cooked through.

4_ Serve the meatballs with couscous, wholemeal pasta or courgetti.

- Leftover meatballs make a great high-protein snack on their own to eat during the day or after a training session.
- The meatballs in sauce can be frozen for 3 months in an airtight container. It may be more convenient to freeze them in smaller batches.

Almond crusted cod loin with lemon and caper yoghurt dressing

Fish is not always a popular food choice. I often think this is because people don't know what to do with it; they believe it will take too long to prepare or is prohibitively expensive. The almond crust on this cod is delicious, and if you don't have any fresh herbs to hand, stick to dried thyme. Frozen fish is just as good, so try cod steaks or any other white fish with the same texture. You can also use this crust on salmon fillets.

SERVES 4

75g ground almonds
25g unsalted butter
1 garlic clove, crushed
Zest of 1 lemon
2 tbsp chopped rosemary, parsley or
    thyme leaves
4 cod loin fillets
Sea salt and black pepper

FOR THE SAUCE
120g Greek yoghurt
1 tbsp lemon juice
1 tbsp capers, chopped
1 tbsp dill, chopped

1_ Preheat the oven to 200°C/180°C fan/Gas 6.
2_ Put the almonds into a bowl. Melt the butter and add to the bowl with the garlic, lemon zest and your herb of choice. Season with salt and pepper, then set aside.
3_ Place the cod loins on a baking tray lined with parchment paper. Spoon the almond crust on top of the fish and press down to cover, then bake in the oven for 15 minutes until the cod flakes to the touch.
4_ While the cod is cooking, prepare the sauce. Place all the ingredients in a small bowl and whisk with a fork. Season with a little salt.
5_ Serve the cod and sauce with a simple salad or mashed potato and green vegetables.

Spelt paella

Paella is a deliciously comforting dish that is best when slightly gloopy and unctuous on the plate. This paella uses spelt, a wholegrain that behaves in a similar way to arborio rice when used in this dish. I have also used frozen seafood as it is cheaper than fresh and works just as well. One of the best bits of paella is the crust at the bottom, called the socarrat. Try to be as gentle as you can with your paella, so you allow this to form in the same way with the spelt.

SERVES 4–6

2 tbsp extra virgin olive oil
2 onions, finely diced
1 red pepper, sliced
1 green pepper, sliced
2 garlic cloves, chopped
1 tbsp tomato purée
2 tsp smoked paprika
300g pearled spelt
600ml Vegetable or Chicken stock
    (see page 215)
Pinch of saffron
Zest and juice of 1 lemon
100g frozen peas
300g skinless and boneless chicken
    thighs, cut into bite-sized pieces
300g frozen raw seafood mix, defrosted
Handful of flat-leaf parsley, chopped
    (optional)
Lemon wedges
Sea salt and black pepper

• This dish will keep in the fridge for up to 2 days. I would not advise freezing this dish as it has been made with frozen seafood; however, if you use a fresh raw seafood mix you can freeze the dish up to for 3 months.

1_ Set a large, deep-sided non-stick frying pan over a medium heat and add the oil. Once hot, add the onions and peppers and fry for 8 minutes until softened. Add the garlic, tomato purée and smoked paprika, then stir and cook for 1 minute more.

2_ Stir the spelt into the pan until the grains are coated in the oil, then add the stock, saffron, lemon zest and juice, peas and chicken. Season with salt and pepper and bring to the boil, then reduce the heat, cover and simmer for 25 minutes until the chicken is cooked and the liquid is nearly absorbed.

3_ Remove the lid and add the seafood but do not stir it in. Place the lid back on the pan and cook for 5 minutes, then turn up the heat for 1 minute. Turn off the heat, remove the lid and scatter with parsley (if using) and top with lemon wedges.

4_ Serve from the pan along with some of the crusted grains that have hopefully baked on the bottom of the pan.

Prawn and salmon burgers with spicy coriander slaw

These burgers are a great way to use up any leftover fish in your fridge or freezer, plus they're not breaded, which keeps them light and fresh. Making your own slaw is a tasty way to get more veggies into your diet, and it also means you can control what goes into it. Shop-bought coleslaws are typically held together with stabilizers such as guar gum and xanthan gum, which prevent ingredients from separating while extending the shelf life.

SERVES 4

3 skinless salmon fillets (about 400g), chopped
180g raw prawns, peeled and chopped
Zest of 1 lemon
1 tsp ground cumin
Pinch of chilli flakes
1 tbsp wholemeal flour
1 tbsp extra virgin olive oil
Sea salt

FOR THE SLAW
4 tbsp natural yoghurt
2 tbsp Mayonnaise (see page 206)
Handful of coriander leaves
1 garlic clove, chopped
Juice of ½ lime
½ green chilli, chopped
½ small red cabbage, finely shredded
2 carrots, peeled and grated
2 spring onions, thinly sliced

TO SERVE
4 Wholemeal rolls (see page 195), toasted, or baked sweet potato wedges

1_ Place half of the salmon, half of the prawns, the lemon zest, cumin, chilli flakes and a pinch of salt in a food processor and blitz to a coarse paste. Transfer the mixture to a bowl and add the remaining salmon and prawns along with the flour.

2_ Mix together well using wet hands or a spatula, then form into 4 patties. Transfer these to a greased baking sheet or plate and chill in the fridge for 15 minutes.

3_ Meanwhile, make the slaw starting with the dressing. Place the yoghurt, mayonnaise, coriander, garlic, lime juice and chilli into a small food processor or blender and blitz until smooth. Now place the cabbage, carrots and spring onions in a large bowl and combine well. Keep the slaw and dressing separately in the fridge until you are ready to serve.

4_ To cook the burgers, heat the oil in a large non-stick frying pan set over a medium-high heat. Once hot, add the burgers to the pan and cook for 3–5 minutes on each side until cooked through (you may need to do this in two batches depending on the size of your pan).

5_ Pour the dressing over the slaw and mix well, then season with a little salt.

6_ Serve the burgers with baked sweet potato wedges or in toasted buns topped with slaw – any remaining slaw can be served on the side.

- You can use frozen fish and seafood but defrost before using.
- These burgers can be frozen raw for 3 months. Defrost thoroughly in the fridge before cooking.

North Indian spiced cottage pie

This is my ultimate comfort dish – it's basically Indian combined with pie! The warming spices of garam masala and turmeric are synonymous with North India, and the addition of red lentils gives a nice texture in combination with the lamb. Frozen veggies are classed as a processed food, believe it or not. Still, in many cases, they are nutritionally superior to fresh as they are flash-frozen shortly after harvesting, which helps to retain their vitamin C content.

SERVES 6

1 tbsp extra virgin olive oil
1 large onion, finely diced
2 garlic cloves, finely chopped
2.5cm piece of fresh ginger, peeled and grated
2 tsp garam masala
½ tsp ground turmeric
1 tsp ground cumin
1 tsp dried chilli flakes
500g minced lamb (10% fat)
400g tin chopped tomatoes
100g red lentils, rinsed and drained
150g frozen peas
1kg Maris Piper potatoes, peeled and cut into small chunks
150ml milk
Knob of butter
Sea salt and white pepper

- This dish can be frozen for up to 3 months but should be cooked first. To cook from frozen, preheat the oven to 180°C/160°C fan/Gas 4 and cook covered in foil for 1½ hours. Increase the heat and take off the foil, then cook for a further 20 minutes to crisp up the top.

1_ Preheat the oven to 200°C/180°C fan/Gas 6.

2_ Set a large, deep-sided non-stick frying pan with a lid over a medium heat and add the olive oil. Once hot, add the onion and fry for 3 minutes until it softens, then add the garlic and ginger and cook for a further 2 minutes. Add the spices to the pan and cook for 1 minute until they become fragrant (add a splash of water if the spices stick).

3_ Add the lamb mince to the pan and cook for 4 minutes, breaking it up as you go and combining well with the spices.

4_ Pour the chopped tomatoes into the pan then fill the tin with water and add that as well. Stir in the red lentils and peas, then season with salt and white pepper. Cover the pan and turn the heat down a little, then cook for 25 minutes, stirring occasionally.

5_ While the lamb is cooking bring a large saucepan of water to the boil. Add the potatoes and cook for about 15 minutes, or until tender. If you want to save time, you can leave the potato skins on – this will add a little more fibre, which is good for your health. Drain the potatoes then put them back in the pan and mash with the milk and butter using a potato masher (it doesn't have to be super smooth).

6_ Once the lamb is cooked, transfer it to a large rectangular ovenproof dish or 6 small dishes. Top the pie with the mash, spreading it to cover the rim of the dish, then bake in the oven for 20 minutes until the topping has a crispy golden crust.

7_ Serve in bowls or on plates with some green vegetables.

Melt-in-the-middle salmon and cod fishcakes

Making the sauce in these fishcakes yourself means removing the modified starches and inverted sugar syrups used in shop-bought fishcakes. This recipe also uses a wholemeal crumb to coat the cakes and there is no deep-frying, which improves the nutrient profile. Serve with steamed green veggies.

SERVES 4

500g Maris Piper potatoes, peeled and cut into small pieces
300g skinless cod fillet
120g skinless salmon fillet
Pinch of freshly grated nutmeg
2 tbsp milk
Handful of fresh flat-leaf parsley, finely chopped
Zest of 1 lemon
3 tbsp wholemeal flour
2 eggs, beaten
100g fresh breadcrumbs
2 tbsp extra virgin olive oil

FOR THE SAUCE
1 tbsp wholemeal flour
1 tbsp butter
300ml milk
50g mature Cheddar cheese, grated
1 tsp Dijon mustard
Sea salt and black pepper

- These fishcakes can be frozen for up to 1 month once coated in breadcrumbs. To cook, defrost first in the fridge for 2 hours, then follow step 8 in the method.

1_ Make the sauce at least 2 hours in advance, so it has time to freeze. Put the flour and butter into a small saucepan set over a low heat and stir to make a paste as the butter melts.

2_ Slowly pour the milk into the pan and whisk until a smooth sauce forms. Keep whisking for a further 5 minutes until the sauce thickens. Remove the pan from the heat then stir in the cheese and mustard. Season with a little salt and pepper. Divide the mixture evenly between 4 silicone cupcake cases then place in the freezer for at least 2 hours.

3_ Boil the potatoes in a large saucepan of salted water for about 15 minutes until tender, then remove with a slotted spoon and leave to dry.

4_ Place the fish in the same pan of water and poach for 5–6 minutes until cooked. Remove the fish from the same pan then set aside to cool; once cool flake the fish into chunks.

5_ Transfer the potatoes to a clean pan. Add the nutmeg and milk then mash until smooth. Now add the fish, parsley and lemon zest and fold together. Set aside to cool.

6_ Divide the fishcake mixture into 4 balls and make a well in the centre of each. Take the frozen sauce out of the freezer and push one frozen disc into each of the fishcakes, then shape the potato mixture around it. Place on parchment paper and put in the freezer for 20 minutes.

7_ Coat each fishcake in flour, then dip in the egg and then the breadcrumbs to cover.

8_ Preheat the oven to 200°C/180°C fan/Gas 6. Heat the oil in a non-stick frying pan over a medium heat, then cook the fishcakes on each side for 3 minutes until browned. Transfer to a baking sheet and cook in the oven for 15 minutes until the centres are hot.

9_ Serve with salad, peas or fine green beans.

Pork and pineapple skewers with citrus couscous

Griddled or barbecued meat often works well with fruit; and pineapple and pork is a delicious combination. Pineapple also contains a type of enzyme called bromelain, which helps break down protein. Honey, tamari and vinegar make the perfect salty and sweet dressing that works well with the orange juice in the couscous. Although technically a processed food, tinned fruit is still healthy, especially when tinned in juice. The process does reduce the amount of vitamin C in the fruit but it is a convenient alternative to fresh.

SERVES 4 (MAKES 8 KEBABS)

250g wholemeal couscous
500ml hot fresh Chicken stock or
    Vegetable stock (see page 215)
2 tbsp extra virgin olive oil
Juice of 1 orange
2 handfuls of chopped herbs (coriander,
    mint or parsley)
Handful of pistachio kernels, roughly
    chopped
Pinch of chilli flakes (optional)
4 tbsp honey
4 tbsp apple cider vinegar
2 tsp tamari
600g lean pork fillet, cut into bite-sized
    cubes
300g pineapple chunks (fresh or tinned
    in juice)
1 green pepper, deseeded and cut into
    squares
6 spring onions, trimmed and cut into
    4 pieces
Sea salt and black pepper

1_ If you are using wooden skewers, soak 8 skewers in cold water (this prevents them from burning on the grill).

2_ Put the honey, vinegar and tamari into a small saucepan set over a low heat and warm through, then leave to cool. Tip the cubed pork into the pan and mix well so that all the pieces are well covered in the sauce. Leave to marinate for 15 minutes.

3_ Put the couscous into a large shallow bowl and pour over the stock. Cover and leave to sit for 5 minutes until fluffy. Add the olive oil and orange juice then season with salt and pepper and fluff up with a fork. Stir in the herbs, pistachio kernels and chilli flakes, then set aside.

4_ Build your kebabs by alternating the skewers with pieces of pork, pineapple, green pepper and spring onion.

5_ Heat a griddle pan or large non-stick frying pan set over a high heat. You can also barbecue these skewers in the summer.

6_ Griddle the skewers for 3 minutes each side (12 minutes in total) until the pork is cooked through. If they start to burn, turn them more regularly.

7_ Serve the skewers on top of the couscous.

Beef and vegetable pie with wholemeal pastry

There is nothing more comforting and moreish than a beef pie. However, the quality of shop-bought pies can vary greatly and some brands contain modified starches and emulsifiers to improve the texture and shelf life. Even when you make your own, using stock cubes introduces flavour enhancers such as monosodium glutamate and disodium guanylate, so it's better to choose fresh stock. Working with wholemeal pastry can be tricky, but a rustic look to a homemade pie is even more appealing.

SERVES 6

1 tbsp extra virgin olive oil
600g skirt steak, sliced into strips
1 large onion, finely chopped
2 carrots, peeled and finely diced
2 celery sticks, finely diced
100g button mushrooms, halved
2 garlic cloves, chopped
2 tbsp wholemeal flour
1 tbsp tomato purée
½ tsp ground cinnamon
500ml fresh beef or Chicken stock
   (see page 215)
Sea salt and black pepper

FOR THE PASTRY
400g plain wholemeal flour, plus extra
   for dusting
200g butter
6–8 tbsp cold water
1 egg, beaten

• The pie/pies can be frozen before you bake them and stored for up to 3 months in the freezer. Defrost before cooking and bake as above.

1_ Set a heavy-based pan with a lid over a medium heat and add the oil. When hot, add the steak in batches; once browned remove from the pan and set aside.

2_ Add the onion, carrot, celery and mushrooms to the pan and cook for 5 minutes. Add a splash of water as you go to help the vegetables to soften.

3_ Add the garlic and flour then stir for 1 minute. Now add the steak, tomato purée, cinnamon, stock and 250ml water. Bring to the boil, then cover and simmer gently for 1 hour until the meat is tender, stirring occasionally.

4_ While the meat is cooking, start preparing the pastry. Place the flour and butter in a food processor and pulse gently until the mixture resemble fine breadcrumbs. You can also do this with your hands by rubbing the flour and butter together through your fingers. Add enough of the water to form a dough then cover and set aside.

5_ Preheat the oven to 200°C/180°C fan/Gas 6.

6_ Remove the lid off the pan after 1 hour and season to taste with salt and pepper. Transfer to a 2-litre pie dish (or 6 individual pie dishes) and set aside.

7_ Transfer the dough to a clean, lightly floured work surface and roll out to a thickness of about 3–5mm.

8_ Drape the pastry over the beef mixture and trim any excess then crimp using a fork. Brush the top with the beaten egg and bake in the oven for 30 minutes until the pastry has coloured and is crisp to the touch.

9_ Remove the pie from the oven and serve with green peas.

Spicy prawns with creamy cherry tomato sauce and courgetti

This dish is excellent for people trying to eat fewer carbohydrates, as it substitutes spaghetti for courgette noodles (courgetti). Frozen seafood is technically processed but should be viewed as healthy and often cheaper than buying fresh (it also saves on food waste if you don't use the whole pack). You can prepare your courgetti in large batches and store it with a squeeze of lemon juice in a sealed container in the fridge for up to 5 days.

SERVES 2

3 tbsp extra virgin olive oil
1 small red onion, finely diced
2 garlic cloves, finely diced
200g cherry tomatoes
½ red chilli, deseeded and thinly sliced
Juice of ½ small lemon
180g frozen raw king prawns, defrosted
2 tbsp Greek yoghurt
Small handful of fresh basil leaves
Sea salt
3 large courgettes, cut into noodles with a julienne peeler or spiralizer

- If you have herbs left over, a clever tip is to half fill an ice-cube tray with water, then add your chopped herb of choice to each cube and push it in as much as possible. Once the cube is frozen, top the tray with more water and freeze again. Transfer the cubes to labelled sealable containers (one for each different herb). When you are cooking, just pop a few cubes into your dish.

1_ Set a large saucepan over a medium-high heat and add all but a teaspoon of the oil. Once the oil is hot add the onion and fry for 3 minutes until softened.

2_ Add the garlic, tomatoes and chilli to the pan and cook for a further 5 minutes until the cherry tomatoes soften and colour the oil slightly orange. Add the lemon juice and 2 tablespoons of water to the pan, then stir to deglaze.

3_ Add the prawns to the pan and cook for 3 minutes until they turn pink. Take the pan off the heat and stir in the yoghurt and basil leaves, then season with salt. Place some foil over the pan to keep the sauce warm.

4_ Set a large non-stick frying pan over a high heat and add the remaining teaspoon of oil. Once the pan is hot add the courgette noodles and gently stir-fry for 1–2 minutes until they become tender.

5_ To serve, divide the courgetti between 2 plates and top with the sauce.

Everyday Meals

Grilled salmon, potato and basil salad with raspberry vinaigrette

Fresh fish, especially oily fish, is the perfect healthy food and you should aim to include a couple of servings a week to get a good dose of those omega-3 fatty acids. This salad is a tasty way to eat salmon and works well with the raspberry vinaigrette. Making your own vinaigrette means avoiding ultra-processed ingredients such as xanthan gum (used as a stabilizer) and preservatives such as potassium sorbate.

SERVES 2

250g new potatoes
160g fine French beans, trimmed
2 skinless salmon fillets
1 small orange
60g mixed salad leaves or rocket
Handful of basil leaves, torn
4 tbsp Raspberry vinaigrette
   (see page 210)

1_ Bring a saucepan of water to the boil, then add the potatoes and boil for 10–15 minutes until tender. In the final few minutes of cooking, add the beans. Drain and rinse under cold water, then set aside to cool.

2_ Heat the grill to medium. Place the salmon fillets on a baking tray, then grill for 5–7 minutes until cooked (the salmon should flake easily when tested with a knife).

3_ While the salmon is cooking, prepare the salad. Halve the orange and juice one half, then remove the peel and pith from the other half and cut into slices.

4_ Cut the potatoes in half and add to a bowl with the French beans, salad leaves, herbs and orange juice. Toss together, then drizzle over the raspberry vinaigrette.

5_ Allow the salmon to cool a little before flaking over the salad.

- This dish would also work well with trout or mackerel.
- You can also serve this dish with Everyday dressing (see page 207).

Vegan & Vegetarian

Spicy bean burgers with lime yoghurt

The Burger King spicy bean burger was my choice of takeaway when I was younger, so I thought it would be fun to try and recreate it. This version has lime yoghurt instead of mayonnaise to add a bit of freshness. The original burger contained a lot of salt, which you will reduce dramatically when making this dish yourself.

SERVES 4

1 tbsp extra virgin olive oil
1 red onion, finely chopped
2 garlic cloves, finely chopped
480g dried red kidney beans, soaked and
  cooked (see page 64)
1 egg, beaten
50g wholemeal breadcrumbs
2 tsp ground cumin
1 tsp ground coriander
1 tsp smoked paprika
1–2 tsp cayenne pepper
½ tsp sea salt
Zest and juice of 1 lime
150g Greek yoghurt
4 fresh Wholemeal rolls or Wholemeal
  pitta breads (see pages 195 and 194),
  toasted
4 tbsp Tomato ketchup (see page 199)
4 slices of Edam cheese (optional)
1 large beef tomato, sliced
Iceberg lettuce

1_ Preheat the oven to 200°C/180°C fan/Gas 6. Line a baking sheet with parchment paper.

2_ Set a large non-stick frying pan over a medium-high heat and add the oil. Once hot, add the onion and fry for 3 minutes until softened. Add the garlic and fry for a further 2 minutes, then take the pan off the heat.

3_ Place the beans in a large bowl and crush with a potato masher until they are roughly crushed (you can also pulse them in a food processor). Tip the onion and garlic into the bowl along with the egg, breadcrumbs, spices, salt and half of the lime juice. Using your hands, mix everything together until well combined, then mould the mixture into 4 burger-shaped patties.

4_ Place the patties on the baking sheet and cook for 15–20 minutes, carefully turning them halfway through.

5_ While the burgers are cooking combine the yoghurt with the lime zest and remaining lime juice, and add a pinch of salt.

6_ To build you burger, spread the bottom part of the bun with the homemade ketchup and the top part with the lime yoghurt. Place the burger in the bun topped with cheese (if using), tomato and lettuce. Serve alone or with potato wedges and salad.

- You can use 2 x 400g tins kidney beans in this recipe (rinsed and drained) instead of dried.
- If you don't have homemade ketchup, then try making a tomato salsa (see page 144) to use instead.
- You can freeze the burgers for 3 months before cooking them. Place sheets of parchment paper between them in an airtight container and defrost thoroughly before cooking.

Vegan & Vegetarian

Roasted red pepper, avocado and refried bean quesadillas

These vegan quesadillas can be eaten as a light lunch, served cold, taken to work, or put in the school lunchbox. Try serving them with homemade tomato salsa (see page 144). Refried beans are very easy to make and I urge you to make your own Wholemeal tortillas too (see page 190); they really do make the difference to both the taste and your intake of ultra-processed food ingredients.

SERVES 2

1 large red pepper, halved
1 tbsp extra virgin olive oil, plus extra
    for drizzling
100g dried black beans, soaked and
    cooked (see page 64)
1 small onion, finely chopped
2 garlic cloves, finely chopped
1 tsp ground cumin
½ tsp smoked paprika
½ tsp dried oregano
4 Wholemeal tortillas (see page 190)
Handful of baby spinach leaves
1 avocado, halved and thinly sliced
1 jalapeño chilli pepper (or green chilli),
    thinly sliced
Small handful of coriander, chopped
Juice of 1 lime
Sea salt

- Make a batch of wholemeal tortillas (see page 190) and keep them in the freezer. Transfer to the fridge to defrost or use the defrost setting on the microwave for 30 seconds or so.
- You can use 1 x 400g tin black beans in this recipe (rinsed and drained) instead of dried.

1_ Preheat the oven to 220°C/200°C fan/Gas 7.

2_ Place the pepper halves cut side down on a baking sheet and drizzle with a little oil. Roast in the oven for about 30 minutes until the skin is shrivelled.

3_ Meanwhile, make the refried beans. Either mash the beans with a splash of water in a bowl using a potato masher or fork or blitz them in a blender, depending on how smooth you want them. Set aside.

4_ Set a large non-stick frying pan over a medium heat and add the tablespoon of oil. Once hot, add the onion and cook for 3 minutes until soft and golden. Add the garlic, spices and oregano and fry for 1 minute more. Tip the beans into the pan and stir, then add a splash of water. Cook the beans for 3–4 minutes and stir frequently until heated through, adding more liquid if they get too thick (they need to be spreadable). Season with salt then take off the heat to cool.

5_ Remove the pepper from the oven and leave to cool. Once cooled slice into two lengthways.

6_ Place the tortillas on a flat work surface and spread with the refried beans. Add baby spinach leaves, slices of red pepper and avocado, then sprinkle with jalapeños and coriander. Squeeze half a lime over each one and season with a good pinch of salt, then fold the filled tortillas over in half.

7_ Place a snug-fitting piece of parchment paper in a large frying pan, set over a high heat, then transfer one quesadilla to the pan and cook for 1 minute on each side. Repeat for the second quesadilla. Cut them in half and serve warm.

Smoky bean shakshuka

Everyone should know how to make a good shakshuka as it is a highly nutritious and cost-effective meal you can serve any time of day. This recipe uses black beans, which add nutrients such as magnesium, iron and zinc to the dish – as well as plant protein. Tinned beans are a processed food that is considered healthy, and I would rather someone eat beans and pulses than avoid them because they had to soak them overnight. Look for tinned beans and pulses that contain just water and give them a good rinse before you use them.

SERVES 2

1 tbsp extra virgin olive oil
1 large onion, finely chopped
1 large red pepper, thinly sliced
2 garlic cloves, crushed
2 tsp smoked paprika
1 tsp ground cumin
1 tbsp tomato purée
400g tin chopped tomatoes
200g dried black beans, soaked and
   cooked (see page 64)
4 eggs
Handful of flat-leaf parsley, chopped
Sea salt and black pepper

1_ Set a large, deep-sided non-stick frying pan over a medium heat and add the oil. Once hot add the onion and pepper and cook for 6–8 minutes to soften.

2_ Add the garlic, spices and tomato purée, then cook for 2 minutes. Tip the tomatoes and beans into the pan, then simmer gently with the lid on for 10 minutes. Remove the lid and season to taste with salt and pepper, then cook for a further 2 minutes to allow the sauce to thicken.

3_ Use a spoon to make 4 deep wells in the mixture. Crack an egg into each one, then cover the pan and reduce the heat to low-medium. Cook the eggs for 5 minutes until the egg whites are cooked through but the yolks are still runny.

4_ Scatter with parsley and serve in bowls with chunks of Seeded wholemeal and rye loaf (see page 191).

• You can use 2 x 400g tins of black beans (rinsed and drained) in place of dried.

Vegan & Vegetarian

Broccoli, tofu and shiitake mushroom broth

There is something very nurturing about an Asian-flavoured broth, and the shiitake mushrooms in this dish give it a moreish umami flavour. Making your own vegetable stock is an excellent way to use vegetables and herbs in your fridge, while at the same time avoiding flavour enhancers like monosodium glutamate and other ultra-processed ingredients like hydrolyzed soya protein.

SERVES 4

1 tsp extra virgin olive oil
   200g broccoli, cut into small florets
1 tbsp sesame oil
2.5cm piece of fresh ginger, peeled and grated
1 small red chilli, thinly sliced
100g shiitake mushrooms
150g firm tofu, cut into small cubes
1 litre Vegetable stock (see page 215)
2 tbsp tamari
1 tbsp white or yellow miso paste
1 tbsp rice wine vinegar
1 tbsp honey or maple syrup
1 head of Chinese leaf, finely shredded
1 spring onion, thinly sliced
Small handful of coriander leaves

1_ Set a large non-stick frying pan over a high heat and add the olive oil. Add the broccoli to the pan and cook for 2 minutes, being careful not to move it around the pan too much so it chars slightly. Remove the broccoli from the pan and set aside.

2_ Heat the sesame oil in a large non-stick saucepan set over a high heat, then add the ginger and chilli and cook for 1 minute. Add the mushrooms and tofu and cook for a further 2 minutes, tossing and stirring the mixture gently so the tofu doesn't break up.

3_ Turn the heat down to medium and add the stock, tamari, miso paste, vinegar and honey. Simmer for 5 minutes, then add the Chinese leaf and simmer for a further 1 minute, so it stays crunchy.

4_ Serve the broth in bowls and garnish with the sliced spring onion and coriander leaves.

Easy vegan pho with soba noodles

There is something deeply satisfying and nourishing about a big bowl of noodles in broth. There are quite a few ingredients to this dish but they are mostly there to flavour the broth. Shop-bought noodles in broth are usually dried and contain flavour enhancers (E621, also known as monosodium glutamate), hydrolyzed maize protein, dextrose and colourings such as E150c, which is a caramel colour made by controlled heating of carbohydrate sources with food-grade ammonium compounds. If you don't know what these compounds are (and don't want to eat them), then I'm sure you'll agree it's worth taking the time to make your pho from scratch.

SERVES 4–6

250g soba noodles
2 litres Vegetable stock (see
    page 215)
1 onion, quartered
3 garlic cloves, halved
2 star anise
2 cloves
2.5cm piece of fresh ginger, peeled and
    cut into matchsticks
1 cinnamon stick
1 red chilli, halved
250g mushrooms quartered
2 tbsp tamari (or more to taste)
Small handful of coriander (leaves and
    stalks), roughly chopped
Small handful of mint leaves
4 spring onions, shredded lengthways
300g beansprouts
1 red chilli, thinly sliced
Handful of raw peanuts, chopped
    (optional)
1 lime, quartered

1_ Bring a saucepan of water to the boil. Add the soba noodles and boil for 4–5 minutes. Drain and rinse under cold water, then set aside.

2_ Put the stock, 500ml water, onion, garlic, star anise, cloves, ginger, cinnamon, chilli and mushrooms into a large saucepan and bring to a simmer. Cover the pan and leave to simmer for 20 minutes. Take the saucepan off the heat and add the tamari.

3_ To serve, remove the star anise, cloves and cinnamon with a slotted spoon, then divide the noodles between 4 deep bowls then top each with coriander, mint, spring onions and beansprouts. Ladle the broth over the noodles in the bowls, leaving the onion and garlic in the pan.

4_ Garnish with the sliced chilli, peanuts and lime wedges.

- For extra spice you could serve with homemade hot sauce (see page 209).
- You can make up a batch of the aromatic broth and store in the freezer in an airtight container for up to 3 months.

Vegan & Vegetarian

Roasted mushrooms on toast with tarragon avonnaise

Mushrooms have a meaty texture and are rich in glutamate, also known as umami, giving them a savoury flavour. Many ultra-processed foods use the flavour enhancer monosodium glutamate (MSG) to create this taste. This vegan-friendly avocado 'mayonnaise' is really versatile; for this recipe, it is combined with tarragon, which works well with mushrooms.

SERVES 2

6 portobello mushrooms (or 400g mixed mushrooms)
3 garlic cloves, finely chopped
1 tbsp rosemary leaves, finely chopped
2 tbsp extra virgin olive oil
1 tbsp balsamic vinegar
2 slices of fresh wholemeal bread, such as Seeded wholemeal and rye loaf (see page 191)

FOR THE TARRAGON AVONNAISE
½ batch of Vegan avonnaise (see page 206)
2 tbsp tarragon leaves
Pinch of sea salt

1_ Preheat the oven to 200°C/180°C fan/Gas 6.
2_ Scatter the mushrooms into a baking tray in a single layer and then roast in the oven for 15 minutes.
3_ While the mushrooms are cooking mix the garlic, rosemary, olive oil and balsamic vinegar in a small cup. Remove the mushrooms from the oven and drain off all the liquid. Pour the dressing over the mushrooms and season with salt, then toss and return to the oven to roast for a further 10 minutes.
4_ Meanwhile, make the tarragon avonnaise by adding all the ingredients to a small food processor and blitzing until smooth.
5_ Remove the mushrooms from the oven and set aside while you toast the bread.
6_ Spread the avonnaise on the toast and then lay the mushrooms on top.

Sag chana with avocumber dressing

You can use tinned chickpeas in this vegan curry to save time soaking them. Tinned chickpeas can be viewed as a healthy processed food, they have many health benefits and you can also make use of the aquafaba from tinned chickpeas as a substitute for egg white in vegan recipes. Ready-made or takeaway curries are often artificially thickened but in traditional Indian cuisine spinach is often used as a thickener. What really makes this dish is the freshness of the cucumber and avocado (avocumber) dressing.

SERVES 4

1 tbsp extra virgin olive oil
1 large onion, finely diced
2 garlic cloves, chopped
2.5cm piece of fresh ginger, peeled and
    chopped
2 tbsp medium curry powder
½ tsp ground turmeric
480g dried chickpeas, soaked and cooked
    (see page 64)
2 large handfuls of spinach
1 cucumber, peeled and seedy core
    removed
1 large avocado
Juice of 1 lime
Handful of fresh coriander
Sea salt and black pepper

1_ Heat the oil in a large saucepan set over a medium heat.
2_ Add the onion and fry for 5 minutes until softened, then add the garlic and ginger and cook for 1 minute.
3_ Add the curry powder, turmeric and a tablespoon of water and cook for 30 seconds until fragrant, stirring to coat the onion in the spices.
4_ Add the chickpeas, spinach and 500ml water and bring to a simmer, then cook for about 10 minutes until the mixture has thickened. Season to taste with salt and pepper.
5_ While the chickpeas are cooking, place the cucumber, avocado, lime juice and coriander in a small food processor or blender and blitz until smooth. Season with salt.
6_ Serve the curry in bowls with a dollop of the avocumber dressing.

- You can use 2 x 400g tins of chickpeas in this recipe (rinsed and drained) instead of dried.

Tofu traybake with green goddess dressing

Although tofu is a processed food it is not considered detrimental to health. This is a quality source of protein for vegans because it contains all the essential amino acids. The hero of this dish is the goddess dressing, which is mellow and citrusy with the addition of fresh herbs. If you don't like butternut squash, you can replace it with sweet potatoes, which will cook in less time. Look out for British asparagus, which is in season during May and June.

SERVES 4

400g extra-firm tofu
2 tbsp tamari
1 tbsp honey or maple syrup
1 tsp sesame oil
500g butternut squash, peeled and cut
    into 1.5cm cubes
4 garlic cloves
1 small red onion, cut into 6 pieces
3 tbsp extra virgin olive oil
200g broccoli, cut into small florets
200g thick asparagus, base trimmed
    and cut into 3 pieces
80g frozen peas, defrosted
Sea salt and black pepper

FOR THE GREEN GODDESS DRESSING
1 batch of Tahini dressing (see page 207)
Large handful of fresh mixed herbs such
    as basil, coriander and parsley

1_ Preheat the oven to 200°C/180°C fan/Gas 6.
2_ Wrap the tofu in kitchen paper and squeeze it to remove the excess water. Repeat until the tofu is dry, then cut into slices and place in a shallow bowl.
3_ Combine the tamari, honey and sesame oil in a small cup, then pour over the tofu and leave to marinate for 20 minutes.
4_ Put the butternut squash, garlic and onion into a deep-sided baking tray and add 2 tablespoons of the olive oil. Put the tray in the oven and roast for 30–35 minutes until the squash is tender. Turn once while roasting.
5_ Place the broccoli and asparagus in a bowl and coat with the remaining tablespoon of olive oil.
6_ Remove the butternut squash from the oven, transfer to a bowl and set aside, then add the broccoli, asparagus and marinated tofu to the baking tray and put in the oven to roast for 10 minutes.
7_ Tip the peas into the baking tray and cook for a further 3 minutes in the oven.
8_ Meanwhile, prepare the green goddess dressing by adding all the ingredients to a blender and blitzing until smooth.
9_ Remove the baking tray from the oven. Add the squash and red onion mixture to the tray, season with salt and pepper and combine well.
10_ Drizzle the dressing over the vegetables before serving.

Middle Eastern spiced aubergine and lentil stew with tahini dressing and pomegranate

This unctuous vegan stew is absolutely delicious but is taken to a whole other level when you add the tahini dressing to it. Lentils are a cost-effective way to make a nutritious meal as they are high in protein and minerals such as zinc and iron, which can be lacking in a vegan diet. Tomato purée is technically a processed food but can be viewed as healthy because of its high levels of the antioxidant lycopene – it is also essential in this dish to add a savoury umami flavour.

SERVES 6

150g red lentils
4 tbsp extra virgin olive oil
3 aubergines, cut into 2.5cm chunks (about 900g)
1 large onion, finely diced
2 courgettes, halved lengthways and sliced into half-moons
400g vine tomatoes, chopped
2 garlic cloves, crushed
2 tbsp tomato purée
1 tbsp ras el hanout
Zest and juice of 1 lime
Handful of dill, finely chopped
Handful of flat-leaf parsley, finely chopped
1 batch of Tahini dressing (see page 207)
80g pomegranate seeds
Sea salt and black pepper

1_ Place the lentils in a sieve, rinse under cold water, then set aside.

2_ Set a large, deep-sided non-stick frying pan over a medium heat and add 3 tablespoons of the oil. Once hot, add the aubergine and move around the pan to coat in the oil, then add a splash of water. Place the lid on the pan and sweat for 12 minutes, stirring occasionally. Once soft, transfer the aubergine to a plate.

3_ Add the remaining tablespoon of oil to the pan and add the onion, courgettes, tomatoes and garlic. Put the lid back on the pan and sweat slowly for 10 minutes until softened.

4_ Remove the lid then add the tomato purée and ras el hanout and cook for 1 minute, stirring frequently.

5_ Tip the aubergines back into the pan along with the lentils and stir together, then pour in 800ml boiling water. Bring the stew to a simmer, then cover and reduce the heat, simmering gently for 10 minutes. Remove the lid and cook for a further 10 minutes.

6_ Take the pan off the heat and add the lime zest and juice, dill (reserve a few fronds to garnish) and parsley and stir. Season with salt and black pepper.

7_ Serve the stew in bowls and drizzle over the tahini dressing. Garnish with fronds of dill and pomegranate seeds.

8_ You can also serve this stew with Wholemeal pitta breads (see page 194).

• You can freeze this stew for up to 6 months in a sealable container.

Tomato and mascarpone pearl barley risotto

Pearl barley is a wholegrain and the perfect substitute for white arborio rice as it still develops the oozy consistency that makes risotto so moreish. This recipe uses tinned tomatoes, which although technically processed, are a rare example of when processed may be an advantage. Processed tomatoes (tinned, puréed, or sun-dried) contain a lot more of the antioxidant lycopene, which is made available once you break down the cell walls of the fruit.

SERVES 4

1 tbsp olive oil
1 large onion, finely chopped
1 celery stick, finely diced
2 garlic cloves, finely chopped
300g pearl barley
2 x 400g tins cherry tomatoes
2 tbsp tomato purée
1 tsp honey
1 tsp dried oregano
2 tbsp mascarpone
Handful of basil leaves
Sea salt and black pepper

1_ Set a large, deep-sided non-stick frying pan with a lid over a medium heat and add the oil. Once hot, add the onion and celery and cook for 3 minutes until softened. Add the garlic and cook for a further 2 minutes.

2_ Stir in the pearl barley, tinned tomatoes, tomato purée, honey and oregano. Fill both of the empty tomato tins with water and add to the pan.

3_ Bring to the boil, then turn down the heat and simmer gently for 40 minutes, stirring occasionally until the barley is tender. It should still be a bit wet when ready.

4_ Season with salt and pepper, then take off the heat and stir through the mascarpone and basil leaves, reserving some basil to garnish.

5_ Serve the risotto in deep bowls, garnished with a few basil leaves.

• Vegans can switch the honey for maple syrup and leave out the mascarpone. You could add a few tablespoons of Coconut milk (see page 203) to the dish for added creaminess. If you are using tinned coconut milk instead of making your own, do look for one that is just coconut and water without added emulsifiers or thickeners.

Vegan & Vegetarian

Asian chopped salad with sweet potato and miso dressing

This generous serving of veggies in one dish couldn't be more unprocessed even if it tried. The hero of this dish is the addictive sweet potato and miso dressing, which is incredibly moreish. The dressing takes a little time to prepare as you must roast the sweet potatoes.

SERVES 2

50g raw cashew nuts
1 head of Chinese cabbage or cos lettuce, finely shredded
½ red onion, thinly sliced
80g lentil sprouts
1 tbsp mixed seeds
100g frozen edamame beans, defrosted
100g mangetout, sliced lengthways
4 radishes, thinly sliced
1 celery stick, sliced
½ red pepper, thinly sliced
2–3 tbsp Sweet potato and miso dressing (see page 210)

1_ Preheat the oven to 180°C/160°C fan/Gas 4.
2_ Place the cashew nuts on a non-stick baking sheet and place in the oven to cook for 8–10 minutes until golden. Once cooked remove from the oven and set aside to cool.
3_ Once the cashew nuts have cooled, transfer them to a large bowl with the cabbage, onion, lentil sprouts, seeds, edamame, mangetout, radish, celery and red pepper and combine well.
4_ Add the dressing and mix to combine, then serve in bowls.

- The dressing can be batch-cooked and used in many different ways, so if you like it, make it in bulk and keep it in the fridge.

Charred oyster mushroom kebabs with tamari and honey

Oyster mushrooms have just the right texture to turn them into a satisfying meal. This rich Asian-flavoured dressing tastes incredible when you char the mushrooms on a hot griddle or barbecue in the summer. The savoury taste you get from mushrooms is called umami, which translates as 'essence of deliciousness' in Japanese and is regarded as the fifth taste.

SERVES 2
(MAKES 6 SMALL SKEWERS)

25ml tamari
25ml honey or maple syrup
2 tsp sesame oil
3 tbsp light olive oil
2 garlic cloves, finely chopped
500g oyster mushrooms
Little gem lettuce, leaves separated
    and washed
1 tsp sesame seeds, toasted
2 spring onions, thinly sliced

1_ Soak 6 skewers in cold water to prevent them from burning.
2_ Combine the tamari, honey, sesame oil, olive oil and garlic in a large bowl.
3_ Cut the tops off the oyster mushrooms and tear each one into 4 strips lengthways. Place the mushrooms in the bowl with the marinade and combine well, then leave for 20 minutes to marinate.
4_ Thread the mushrooms onto the 6 skewers, folding them over as you do so to give them a chewy texture.
5_ Heat a griddle or non-sick frying pan over a high heat and wait until it is smoking hot. Add the skewers to the pan and cook for about 6 minutes, turning regularly so they become charred. Take them out of the pan and drain on kitchen paper.
6_ Arrange the lettuce leaves on a large plate. Place the kebabs on top of the lettuce and scatter over the sesame seeds and spring onions.

Coconut dahl with roasted beetroot

Dahl is the ultimate comfort food; nothing could be more unprocessed than lentils. If you can find fresh curry leaves, they really make a difference to the flavour, but you can also use dried. Using your homemade coconut milk also gives this dahl a fresher coconut flavour, which is not as claggy as tinned varieties containing stabilizers (guar gum and xanthan gum) and emulsifiers (polysorbate 60). Earthy beetroot is also a perfect flavour partner for sweet coconut.

SERVES 4

200g red split lentils
2 tbsp extra virgin olive oil
1 small onion, finely chopped
2 garlic cloves, finely chopped or grated
1 red chilli, finely chopped
Small handful of curry leaves
1 small cinnamon stick
Zest and juice of ½ lemon
1 tsp hot curry powder
½ tsp ground cumin
½ tsp paprika
400ml Coconut milk (see page 203)
4 medium beetroots, peeled and cut into
    1cm chunks
Sea salt

- The dahl can be frozen, topped with the beetroot, for up to 6 months in an airtight container.
- If you find fresh curry leaves then pick the leaves off the stem and freeze to use next time. They will keep for 12 months in a resealable freezer bag or airtight container.

1_ Preheat the oven to 200°C/180°C fan/Gas 6.

2_ Put the lentils in a sieve and rinse several times until the water runs clear.

3_ Set a saucepan over a medium heat and add 1 tablespoon of the oil. Once hot, add the onion to the pan and cook for 5 minutes until softened.

4_ Add the garlic, chilli, curry leaves, cinnamon stick and lemon zest, then cook for 2 minutes before adding the ground spices and cooking for 1 minute more.

5_ Tip the lentils into the pan and stir, then add the coconut milk and 300ml water. Bring to the boil, then reduce the heat and simmer gently for 25–30 minutes, stirring occasionally, until the lentils are soft.

6_ Meanwhile, spread the beetroot chunks out on a non-stick baking tray, drizzle with the remaining tablespoon of oil and sprinkle over a little salt. Roast in the oven for 20 minutes until tender, then remove from the oven and squeeze over the lemon juice. Set aside.

7_ Season the cooked dahl with salt before serving in bowls topped with the roasted beetroot. This is also great with Wholemeal tortillas or Wholemeal pitta breads (see pages 190 and 194) alongside.

Halloumi traybake with everyday dressing

Traybakes make a quick and easy supper dish when feeding the family. This brightly coloured traybake provides more than three servings of fresh, unprocessed vegetables in a single portion. Many shop-bought dressings are ultra-processed, so you are better off making them yourself – here I've used the Everyday dressing on page 207. Feel free to add more halloumi to the plate if you are feeding hungry teenagers!

SERVES 4

1 large red onion, cut into 8 wedges

2 red peppers, chopped into cubes

1 small aubergine, cut into 1cm cubes

1 large courgette, trimmed and chopped into cubes

6 garlic cloves, unpeeled

300g cherry tomatoes

2 tbsp extra virgin olive oil

1 tbsp dried oregano

100g dried butter beans, soaked and cooked (see page 64)

Handful of pitted black olives

250g halloumi cheese, cubed into bite-sized pieces

Handful of basil leaves

1 batch of Everyday dressing (see page 207)

Sea salt and black pepper

1_ Preheat the oven to 240°C/220°C fan/Gas 9.

2_ Scatter the onion, peppers, aubergine, courgette, garlic and tomatoes into a large roasting tray. Make sure they are well spread out, so they roast rather than steam. Drizzle the vegetables with the oil, sprinkle over the oregano and season with plenty of salt and pepper. Place the tray in the oven and roast for 15 minutes.

3_ Take the tray out of the oven, add the butter beans and olives and toss through the vegetables then return to the oven for a further 10 minutes.

4_ When the vegetables have finished roasting preheat the grill to high. Scatter the halloumi over the vegetables and grill for 5 minutes until the halloumi has browned.

5_ Remove the tray from the grill and squeeze the garlic cloves out of their skins. Scatter the soft garlic cloves and basil leaves over the roasted vegetables.

6_ Drizzle the dressing over the vegetables and serve.

- This traybake is great for work the following day with Wholemeal pitta breads (see page 194).
- You can use 1 x 400g tin of butter beans (rinsed and drained) in this recipe instead of dried.
- Try soaking your sliced halloumi in cold water for an hour before using it as this helps prevent it from splitting. It will also remove some of the saltiness from the brining of the cheese.

Feeding the Kids

Fish fingers and Cajun wedges

Everyone has fed their kids fish fingers at some point because they are quick to prepare and eaten with very little fuss. These homemade ones can be made in batches and frozen. Adding grated Parmesan gives the breadcrumbs a savoury flavour that works well with the fish. If your kids don't fancy spiced wedges, try a little salt or dried mixed herbs to flavour them instead.

SERVES 4

1 egg, beaten
85g wholemeal breadcrumbs
25g Parmesan cheese, finely grated
Zest of 1 lemon
1 tsp dried oregano
5 tbsp wholemeal flour
400g skinless white fish (such as cod or
    haddock), sliced into 12 strips each
    2-3cm thick and 10-12cm long
Sea salt and black pepper

FOR THE WEDGES
3 medium baking potatoes, each cut into
    8 wedges lengthways
1 tbsp extra virgin olive oil, plus extra
    for brushing
1 tsp ground cumin
½ tsp ground coriander
½ tsp smoked paprika

1_ Preheat the oven to 200°C/180°C fan/Gas 6. Lightly brush 2 non-stick baking sheets with a little oil.

2_ Start by making the wedges. Lay the potato wedges out on one of the baking sheets, then drizzle over the oil and toss with your hands to coat. Place the spices and a good pinch of salt in a small bowl and mix to combine. Sprinkle the spice mixture over the wedges then bake in the oven for 30 minutes until golden brown and tender.

3_ Now prepare the fish fingers. Place the beaten egg in a shallow dish. Combine the breadcrumbs, Parmesan, lemon zest and oregano in a bowl, season with salt and pepper and combine well. Transfer the breadcrumb mixture to a plate. Set another plate up with the flour.

4_ Dip the fish strips one at a time into the flour and shake off any excess, then dip into the egg and finally the breadcrumbs, making sure they are well coated. Place on the other baking sheet, transfer to the oven and cook for 20 minutes until golden brown.

5_ Serve the fish fingers with the potato wedges and peas.

- You may want to serve with a little homemade Mayonnaise or Tomato ketchup (see pages 206 and 199), or some tzatziki (yoghurt mixed with grated cucumber) as a dip for the fish fingers.
- You can make breadcrumbs from stale Seeded wholemeal and rye loaf or Wholemeal rolls (see pages 191 and 195). Place them in a resealable bag and freeze for up to 3 months.
- These fish fingers can be frozen before cooking and stored in an airtight container for up to 3 months.

Bashed seeded chicken with creamed corn

Breaded chicken always goes down well with kids, but shop-bought nuggets and other varieties can vary in quality. These foods are often made using bits of chicken, while cheaper brands also fill them out with soy protein isolate. Shop-bought breaded chicken items also often contain modified starches and stabilizers such as sodium acid pyrophosphate 28 (E450) and sodium tripolyphosphate (E451). These breaded chicken breasts have been made using wholemeal flour and seeds to improve their nutrient content.

SERVES 4

4 skinless chicken breasts
4 thick slices of wholemeal bread
 (about 300g)
2 garlic cloves, finely chopped
4 tbsp mixed seeds, toasted
2 eggs, beaten
Wholemeal flour
1 tbsp extra virgin olive oil
Sea salt

FOR THE CREAMED CORN
325g tin sweetcorn (no added
 sugar or salt), drained
2 tbsp single cream
20g Parmesan cheese, finely grated

• You can freeze the chicken for up to 3 months: place the raw breaded chicken in a sealable container with pieces of parchment paper between each one. Defrost thoroughly before cooking.

1_ Place the chicken breasts between two pieces of cling film and bash with a rolling pin or heavy-based saucepan until they are about 1cm thick.

2_ Make the breadcrumbs by placing the bread, garlic and seeds in a food processor with a good pinch of salt and blitzing into fairly fine crumbs.

3_ Place the beaten eggs in a shallow bowl and both the wholemeal flour and breadcrumbs on separate plates.

4_ One at a time, dip the chicken breasts into the flour and shake off any excess. Next, dip the floured chicken into the egg and then into the breadcrumbs to cover completely. Set aside on a baking sheet until ready to cook.

5_ Prepare the creamed corn. Place the sweetcorn in a small saucepan with the cream and heat through for 2 minutes. Take the pan off the heat and then use a stick blender to blitz the corn into a semi-smooth consistency. Add the Parmesan and a small pinch of salt and stir gently.

6_ Set a large non-stick frying pan over a medium heat and add the oil. Once hot, add the breaded chicken to the pan and cook for 3 minutes on each side until crisp and golden.

7_ Reheat the creamed corn. Slice up the breaded chicken and serve with the creamed corn and slices of cucumber and halved cherry tomatoes.

Tortilla pizza

These pizzas are quick to prepare and taste really good, so I often make them for a speedy lunch when working from home. Try making your own wholemeal tortillas in batches and freezing them to fully embrace living an unprocessed life. Get the kids involved with this one, as they can explore lots of interesting toppings and even create exciting faces on their tortilla pizzas. They are also great with a raw egg cracked in the middle before you bake them in the oven.

SERVES 2

6–8 tbsp Tomato sauce (see page 202) or Versatile roasted red pepper sauce (see page 200)
1 garlic clove, finely chopped
1 tsp dried oregano
1 tbsp extra virgin olive oil, plus extra for brushing
2 Wholemeal tortillas (see page 190)
60g grated mozzarella
Sea salt

ADDITIONAL TOPPINGS
Sliced peppers
Sweetcorn
Tinned pineapple (in juice)
Mushrooms
Onions
Peas
Frozen spinach
Basil leaves

1_ Preheat the oven to 220°C/200°C fan/Gas 7. Brush a large non-stick baking sheet with a little oil.
2_ Put the tomato sauce, garlic, oregano, olive oil and a pinch of salt into a bowl and combine well to make your pizza sauce.
3_ Place the tortillas on the baking sheet and spread over the pizza sauce, leaving a 1cm border. Scatter over the mozzarella and any additional toppings you wish to add.
4_ Place the pizzas in the oven and bake for 6–8 minutes until the tortilla edges are crisp and the cheese is bubbling.
5_ Serve with salad or chopped raw vegetables like carrots, cucumber and cherry tomatoes.

• If you don't have either of the sauces to hand, then you can use a jar of tomato passata but do read the label first to check for any added ingredients.

Salmon pesto pasta with toasted pine nuts

This dish is always a winner for kids, who generally like the taste of salmon and pesto. Wholemeal pasta is always a better option; it is less processed than white varieties and contains more fibre. However, if you have fussy eaters, then it may be better to switch to white, rather than watch them push the pasta around the plate. Homemade pesto is a lot more flavoursome and takes minutes to prepare.

SERVES 4

2 skinless salmon fillets
240g wholemeal fusilli
5 tbsp Pesto sauce (see page 209)
1 tbsp Greek yoghurt
2 tbsp pine nuts, toasted
Sea salt and black pepper

1_ Preheat the oven to 180°C/160°C fan/Gas 4 and line a baking sheet with parchment paper.
2_ Place the salmon fillets on the baking sheet and season with salt and pepper, then transfer to the oven and bake for 10–15 minutes until cooked through.
3_ Bring a saucepan of water to the boil, add the pasta and cook for 10–12 minutes until tender. Drain the pasta, then tip back into the pan.
4_ Remove the salmon from the oven and flake, then set aside.
5_ Add the pesto sauce and yoghurt to the pasta pan and stir to combine. Check for seasoning.
6_ Tip the salmon into the pan and gently toss to combine.
7_ Serve the salmon pesto pasta on plates or in bowls sprinkled with the toasted pine nuts.

- You can use frozen salmon fillets (defrosted) for this dish; it even works with tinned salmon if you are on a tighter budget.

Egg and red pepper muffins with guacamole

These bites are perfect for little hands as they can be eaten without cutlery. The spinach is optional for fussy eaters, but you can substitute it with a small grated courgette. Most kids like guacamole, which is excellent if you are worried about little appetites, as the healthy fat content makes it quite energy dense. You can buy ready-made fresh guacamole without preservatives but most guacamole dips found in jars or squeezy bottles contain long lists of ingredients, including modified starches, preservatives and stabilizers such as xanthan gum.

MAKES 6

1 tbsp extra virgin olive oil, plus extra
    for greasing
½ onion, finely diced
½ red pepper, finely diced
100g baby leaf spinach (optional)
5 large eggs
Sea salt

FOR THE GUACAMOLE
2 ripe avocados
Juice of 1 lime
¼ onion, finely diced
2 ripe tomatoes, finely chopped
Small handful of coriander, finely
    chopped (optional)

• These muffins will keep in the fridge for 3 days and they can be frozen for up to 3 months. Make sure they are cooled completely then freeze on a baking sheet for 2 hours before transferring to an airtight container.

1_ Preheat the oven to 190°C/170°C fan/Gas 5. Grease 6 holes of a muffin tin with a little olive oil.

2_ Set a non-stick frying pan over a medium heat and add the oil. Once hot, add the onion and red pepper and fry for 5 minutes until softened then transfer to a plate. If you are using spinach, then add this to the pan and cover, then cook for 1–2 minutes so it wilts. Tip the spinach onto kitchen paper to drain, then chop.

3_ Beat the eggs in a bowl and season with salt. Divide the vegetables evenly between the muffin holes then pour over the egg mixture.

4_ Place the muffin tin in the oven and bake for 15 minutes until the egg has set. Remove from the oven and leave to cool while you make the guacamole.

5_ Scoop the avocado flesh into a bowl, add the lime juice and crush with a fork. Add the onion, tomatoes and coriander and fold together.

6_ Serve the muffins warm or at room temperature with a dollop of guacamole.

7_ If you are not serving straight away, then sit one of the avocado stones in the guacamole to keep it fresh.

Chicken chow mein

Noodles are a great dinner option for kids as they are pretty fun to eat. This versatile dish is an excellent way to use up any vegetables in the fridge, as you can add anything you and your kids like. This is also a good way to use frozen vegetables such as peas, mixed vegetables and broccoli. Frozen vegetables are classed as minimally processed foods and, in some cases, can be more nutritious than fresh vegetables as they are picked and frozen at the source, which retains their nutrient content.

SERVES 4

200g wholewheat egg noodles
1 tbsp extra virgin olive oil
1 garlic clove, finely chopped
1 red pepper, thinly sliced
2 spring onions, sliced
50g mushrooms, sliced
Handful of frozen peas, defrosted
Handful of cooked shredded chicken, prawns or tofu
Handful of beansprouts

FOR THE SAUCE
2 tbsp tamari
2 tsp honey
1 tsp Tomato ketchup (see page 199)
Juice of ½ lime

1_ Bring a large saucepan of water to the boil, add the noodles and cook for 5 minutes until tender. Drain the noodles, then rinse under cold water and set aside to cool.

2_ Prepare the sauce by adding all the ingredients to a small bowl and mixing well.

3. Place a large, deep-sided non-stick frying pan or wok over a high heat and add the oil. Once hot, add the garlic and cook for 20 seconds, then add the vegetables and any meat, seafood or tofu and stir-fry for 2–3 minutes. Add the sauce and a splash of water, then stir.

4. Add the beansprouts and noodles to the pan and cook for a further 2 minutes, stirring regularly until everything is combined.

5. Serve in small bowls.

Lentil and sweet potato pie

This nutritious pie is quick to make once you have prepared the lentils, and you can also batch-cook it to make individual portions to freeze. To make a vegan version, sprinkle a little nutritional yeast over the top of the pie instead of the cheese. Nutritional yeast is a processed food made by deactivating the yeast, which gives it a nutty, cheesy flavour. It is rich in vitamin B12, so it counts as a healthy processed food, as vegans struggle to get this nutrient from their diet.

SERVES 4–6

200g dried green lentils, rinsed
    and drained
450g passata
1 large carrot, peeled and finely diced
½ red pepper, finely diced
150g frozen peas, defrosted
2 sweet potatoes, peeled and diced
    (about 600g)
¼ tsp freshly grated nutmeg
100g Cheddar cheese, grated
Sea salt and black pepper

1_ Put the lentils into a large saucepan of cold water, bring to the boil and cook for 10 minutes. Reduce the heat to a low simmer and cook for a further 30 minutes. Drain the lentils and set aside. Add more water to the pan and bring back to the boil.

2_ Place a saucepan over a medium heat and add the lentils, passata, carrot, red pepper, peas and 100ml water. Season and bring to the boil, then reduce the heat to a simmer and cook for 25 minutes until the vegetables are soft, stirring occasionally.

3_ While the sauce is cooking, place the sweet potatoes in the pan of boiling water and cook for 12–15 minutes until tender. Once cooked, drain and return to the pan. Add the nutmeg and mash until smooth.

4_ Preheat the oven to 200°C/180°C fan/Gas 6.

5_ Transfer the lentil mixture to an ovenproof dish or 6 small pie dishes, then top with the mash and sprinkle over the cheese.

6_ Place the pie in the oven and cook for 20 minutes until the top is golden and the cheese has melted.

- You can use 2 x 400g tins green lentils instead of dried to save time. Make sure you rinse them well before adding to the pan.
- This pie can be chilled in the fridge once the topping has been added and will keep for 2 days, or you can freeze at this point for up to 1 month.

Halloumi, sweet potato and cherry tomato skewers

These skewers are brightly coloured and sweet, which is appealing to kids, not to mention the fact you can pick them up and eat them with your hands. Halloumi is a rich source of calcium, important for growing bones and teeth. Try making them with your kids to help get them interested in new foods. If you don't like halloumi, then paneer cheese also works well.

SERVES 4
(MAKES 8 SMALL SKEWERS)

2 sweet potatoes, peeled and cut into
    16 bite-sized chunks
1 tsp olive oil
1 x 250g packet of halloumi, cut into
    16 bite-sized chunks
16 cherry tomatoes

FOR THE MARINADE
1 tbsp honey
Zest and juice of ½ lime
2 tbsp olive oil
Sea salt

1_ Preheat the oven to 200°C/180°C fan/Gas 6 and soak 8 small wooden skewers in water.
2_ Place the sweet potato on a baking tray and drizzle with the oil, then use your hands to turn and coat them in the oil. Roast in the oven for 15 minutes, or until tender but not too soft. Remove from the oven and leave to cool.
3_ Prepare the marinade by adding all the ingredients to a small bowl and whisking to combine.
4_ Preheat the grill to medium.
5_ Thread each skewer with 2 cubes of sweet potato, 2 cubes of halloumi and 2 cherry tomatoes. Brush the marinade over both sides of the skewers, then grill for 5 minutes until the halloumi has started to brown. Turn the skewers once during cooking.
6_ Serve the skewers on their own or with couscous, salad leaves and cucumber slices.

•   As a vegan option you can switch the cheese for tofu. Try coating the tofu in cornflour and sealing in the pan with a little oil and salt before you use it. Replace the honey in the marinade with maple syrup.

Creamy veggie korma

Every parent should have a good curry recipe. A very savoury-tasting curry works well with kids, especially when served with bread to dunk in the sauce, and you can achieve this even with a veggie curry when you use stock, dried spices and just a little yoghurt. Dried spices give a nicer taste than shop-bought pastes, which are often loaded with salt and can taste a tad synthetic as they are thickened with modified starches and gums.

SERVES 4–6

1 tbsp extra virgin olive oil

1 onion, finely diced

1 garlic clove, finely chopped

Thumb-sized piece of fresh ginger, peeled and grated

2 tsp garam masala

1 tsp ground coriander

½ tsp ground turmeric

½ tsp chilli flakes (optional)

800g mixed vegetables (carrots, cauliflower, courgette, red pepper), chopped into small pieces

300ml Vegetable stock (see page 215)

150g frozen peas

2 tbsp natural yoghurt

1_ Set a large saucepan over a medium heat and add the oil. Once hot, add the onion and cook for 5 minutes until softened. Add the garlic and ginger and cook for a further 2 minutes. Now add the spices (leave out the chilli flakes if you prefer less heat) and cook for 1 minute until they become fragrant. Add a splash of water.

2_ Add the mixed vegetables to the pan with a big splash of water and cook for 5 minutes. Stir to combine the vegetables with the spices.

3_ Add the stock and peas and simmer gently for 10 minutes.

4_ Remove the pan from the heat and stir in the yoghurt.

5_ Serve with brown rice or Wholemeal pitta breads (see page 194).

- To make this dish vegan-friendly you can use Coconut milk (see page 203) in place of yoghurt.
- You can also add a tin of chickpeas (rinsed and drained).
- This curry can be frozen for up to 3 months.

Feeding the Kids

Salmon egg fried rice

Brown rice is an unprocessed food with the bran and the germ intact, making it more nutritious and higher in fibre and minerals such as magnesium. Eggs are a very versatile ingredient, and once the rice is cooked, they are used to create a meal in no time, which is crucial when you're feeding kids. To save even more time, freeze rice in small batches for dishes like this one. If you don't have any salmon, it works just as well with white fish or prawns.

SERVES 4

150g brown rice (basmati or short-grain)
2 skinless salmon fillets
1 tbsp extra virgin olive oil
3 spring onions
½ red pepper, deseeded and finely diced
1 small carrot, peeled and finely diced
1 garlic clove, finely chopped
Handful of frozen peas, defrosted
1 tbsp soy sauce
1 tsp honey
3 large eggs, beaten
Small handful of coriander, chopped (optional)

1_ Place the rice in a sieve and rinse through with cold water a few times. Bring a saucepan of water to the boil and add the rice. Cook for 25 minutes until tender, then drain.

2_ Meanwhile, preheat the oven to 180°C/160°C fan/Gas 4. Place the salmon fillets on a non-stick baking tray and cook in the oven for 12–15 minutes until tender. Once cooked, flake with a fork and set aside.

3_ Heat the oil in a large non-stick frying pan or wok. Once hot, add the spring onions, pepper and carrot and fry for 5 minutes until softened. Add the garlic and fry for a further 30 seconds. Now add the cooked rice and peas and stir gently to heat them through and combine with the vegetables.

4_ Put the soy sauce and honey into a small cup and stir to combine, then add to the rice along with the flaked salmon. Gently toss the mixture.

5_ Make a small well in the middle of the pan and pour in the egg. Leave it for about 1 minute so it starts to cook like an omelette. Move the egg gently around the well in the pan to scramble then fold in the rice to combine.

6_ Scatter with a little chopped coriander if you like, before serving in small bowls.

- You can use white basmati if you can't get the kids to eat brown. You can also swap the peas for frozen or tinned sweetcorn – just make sure it has no added salt or sugar.
- If your kids like spicy food, then you could add a little chilli or a few drops of Hot sauce (see page 209).
- Find out how to freeze rice on pages 55-56.

Packed Lunches

Chicken shawarma wrap

This is a popular takeaway meal, especially after a big night out. Often the shawarma kebab is laden with sauces, usually shop-bought and full of thickeners, flavourings and preservatives. The meat used here is thigh, and you can create this at home with the right spice blend and a hot grill. This sauce is an adaptation of the Tahini dressing on page 207 with added yoghurt; it works really well with red onion and pomegranate seeds.

SERVES 4

8 large skinless and boneless
    chicken thighs
Juice of 2 lemons
3 tbsp extra virgin olive oil
3 garlic cloves, crushed
1 tsp smoked paprika
2 tsp ground cumin
1 tsp ground coriander
1 tsp dried chillies
½ tsp ground cinnamon
Sea salt and black pepper

FOR THE SAUCE
1 batch of Tahini dressing (see page 207)
2 tbsp Greek yoghurt

TO SERVE
4 Wholemeal tortillas or Wholemeal
    pitta breads (see pages 190 and 194)
Thinly sliced red onion
Diced cucumber and tomato
Shredded lettuce
Pomegranate seeds (optional)

1_ Put the chicken thighs into a large bowl and season with salt and pepper.

2_ Add the lemon juice, olive oil, garlic, spices, ½ teaspoon salt and some pepper in a small bowl and whisk to combine. Pour this marinade over the chicken thighs and rub together using your hands to fully coat the meat. You can also do this in a sealable bag if you don't want to use your hands. Cover the bowl (or seal the bag) and place in the fridge for 2 hours or overnight.

3_ While the chicken is marinating you can make the dressing. Combine the tahini dressing with the Greek yoghurt and stir to combine, then chill in the fridge until ready to use.

4_ Preheat the grill to medium-high and arrange the marinated chicken thighs on a grill rack or baking sheet. Grill for 10 minutes on each side, or until the chicken is cooked through. Transfer the chicken to a board and slice.

5_ To construct the shawarma, spread the tahini dressing over a wrap or inside a pitta, then add the chicken slices, salad and pomegranate seeds.

• You can freeze the prepared chicken in batches and store in an airtight container for up to 9 months.
• The grilled chicken will keep in the fridge for up to 2 days and can also be used to make a salad, which also works well with the tahini dressing.

Grilled peach and feta couscous salad

Some people are turned off by wholemeal couscous, thinking it takes longer to prepare. All you need to do is add twice as much liquid and you still get a light and fluffy grain. Choosing wholemeal over white varieties is a simple way to help un-process your life and improve the quality of your diet. These grains are rich in fibre with many proven health benefits, including reducing the risk of cardiovascular disease.

SERVES 4

200g wholewheat couscous
400ml hot Vegetable stock (see page 215) or water
4 tbsp extra virgin olive oil, plus extra for brushing
Juice of 1 lemon
1 tsp honey
2 ripe peaches or nectarines
½ cucumber, peeled, deseeded and chopped
150g cherry tomatoes, halved
½ small red onion, finely chopped
150g feta cheese, crumbled
Sea salt and black pepper

1_ Preheat the grill to medium.

2_ Prepare the couscous by adding to a shallow heatproof dish and adding the hot vegetable stock or water. Cover and leave to stand for 5 minutes then fluff up with a fork. Transfer to a large bowl to cool.

3_ Put the olive oil, lemon juice and honey into a small cup and whisk with a fork to combine. Pour the dressing over the couscous, season with salt and pepper and fluff again with a fork to combine.

4_ Halve the peaches and nectarines and remove the stones, then place each half on a baking sheet and brush with a little oil. Place under the grill and cook for 3 minutes on each side until they become slightly browned (you can also use a griddle on the hob). Once cooked, set to one side to cool, then chop into cubes and add to the couscous.

5_ Add the cucumber, tomatoes, red onion and feta then toss to combine. Taste and adjust the seasoning before serving.

- You can store this dish in the fridge for up to 3 days.
- If you can't find peaches or nectarines then try adding fresh or dried fruits like strawberries, apricots, dates or sultanas.

Mexican-inspired frittata with tomato salsa

Frittatas are a complete meal in a slice and easy to take to work for lunch. Not only are eggs rich in protein, they are a source of almost all the nutrients required for the body to function. This Mexican-inspired frittata includes black beans to make it more of a meal and a fresh salsa that you can pack for work in a separate pot. You can also roll slices of this frittata in a wholemeal wrap for lunch with salad – add a drizzle of homemade Hot sauce (see page 209) for an extra kick.

SERVES 4

1 tbsp extra virgin olive oil
1 red pepper, thinly sliced
1 red onion, sliced
½ tsp ground cumin
½ tsp smoked paprika
8 eggs, beaten
50g dried black beans, soaked and
    cooked (see page 64)
1 jalapeño chilli pepper (or green
    chilli), thinly sliced
Sea salt and black pepper

FOR THE SALSA
4 ripe tomatoes (the sweetest ones
    you can find), chopped
½ red onion, finely diced
Handful of coriander, chopped
Juice of 1 lime
Sea salt

1_ Preheat the oven to 180°C/160°C fan/Gas 4.
2_ Set a large (25cm) ovenproof frying pan over a medium heat and add the oil. Once hot, add the red pepper and onion then fry for 3 minutes until softened. Add the spices and cook for 1 minute, then remove from the heat and set aside.
3_ Crack the eggs into a bowl and whisk with a fork. Add the black beans and stir to combine, then season with salt and pepper.
4_ Make sure the pepper and onion are spread evenly in the pan then scatter over the sliced chilli. Pour the egg and bean mixture into the pan and transfer to the oven. Bake for 15 minutes until the egg has set and is just starting to brown.
5_ While the frittata is in the oven, make the salsa by adding all the ingredients to a bowl and combing well with a spoon.
6_ Remove the frittata from the oven and flip onto a plate so that it is pepper side up.
7_ Leave it to cool slightly before eating straight away or cool completely and wrap in foil before transferring to the fridge.

- You can use ½ a 400g tin black beans in this recipe (rinsed and drained) instead of dried.
- This dish can also be served warm for lunch or a light supper with salad leaves. It will keep in the fridge for up to 3 days or the freezer for up to 3 months.
- You could add a little chilli and lime juice to the Versatile roasted red pepper sauce (see page 200) and serve with that, or with a dollop of Vegan avonnaise (see page 206) – if you have any left in the fridge.

Lentil bowl with tahini dressing

This super healthy lunch option has few ingredients but packs a mighty taste punch. Brown rice and puy lentils act as the base of this dish and are completely unprocessed. The mixed herbs make the difference here, and you can use any that you may have frozen (see Tip on page 98). This dish also uses the tahini dressing, which is used in several recipes in this book, so keep any leftovers to save time when making another dish.

SERVES 2

50g puy lentils, rinsed and drained
50g brown rice, rinsed
½ red onion, thinly sliced
Handful of rocket, roughly chopped
Handful of mixed fresh herbs
  (coriander, parsley, mint), chopped
150g cherry tomatoes, halved
2 tbsp golden sultanas
Tahini dressing (see page 207)

1_ Fill a saucepan with water and bring to the boil. Add the lentils and cook for 5 minutes, then add the brown rice and cook for a further 20 minutes until both grain and lentil are tender.

2_ Prepare the dressing if you don't have any ready prepared in the fridge.

3_ Place the rice and lentils into a large bowl with the remaining salad ingredients and toss together.

4_ Drizzle over as much dressing as you like. If you are taking this to work for lunch, then keep the dressing separate until you are ready to eat.

• Try looking for short-grain brown rice from your local health food shop. It can be cheaper – especially if you buy larger bags, and it has a much nicer texture in a cold salad.

Sesame chicken noodles

This high-protein lunchbox is bursting with raw vegetables and gives a generous portion size. Loading up your plate with vegetables is an excellent way to help regulate your blood glucose levels and keep you feeling full through the afternoon. Rather than an overly processed dressing, this one is made from earthy flavoured tahini with zingy lime (you can add some chilli to the dressing if you like it spicy). This recipe also works well with soba noodles made from buckwheat.

SERVES 2

2 wholewheat noodle nests (100g)

1 tbsp olive oil

2 skinless chicken breasts

100ml Chicken or Vegetable stock (see page 215)

1 red pepper, thinly sliced

1 large carrot, peeled and shredded with a julienne peeler

½ cucumber, peeled, deseeded and chopped

50g frozen edamame beans, defrosted

2 tbsp sesame seeds, toasted

Sea salt

FOR THE DRESSING

2 tbsp runny tahini paste

2 tbsp olive oil

3 tbsp warm water

2 tsp tamari

1 tsp sesame oil

Juice of ½ lime

½ small garlic clove, finely chopped

1 tsp honey

1_ Bring a saucepan of water to the boil, then take off the heat. Add the noodles and leave to soak for 5 minutes until tender. Drain the noodles and set aside to cool.

2_ Set a non-stick frying pan with a lid over a medium heat and add the oil. Once hot add the chicken breasts to the pan and season with a little salt, then cook for 5 minutes, turning once. Add the stock, cover the pan and cook for 8–10 minutes until the chicken is cooked through.

3_ Remove the chicken from the pan and place on a chopping board. Shred the chicken by holding the chicken in place with one fork and pulling at it with another fork.

4_ Prepare the dressing by adding all the ingredients to a small jar with a lid and shaking well (or use a food processor).

5_ Put the salad together by placing the noodles, shredded chicken, vegetables and sesame seeds in a large bowl, then toss together. Pour over the dressing and toss again before dividing into 2 airtight containers.

- This salad with last for up to 2 days in the fridge (without the dressing added).
- You can also dress this salad with the Tahini dressing or Sweet potato and miso dressing (see pages 207 and 210).
- You can swap the wholewheat noodles for soba or lentil, but they will require more cooking time (refer to the packet instructions).

Herby quinoa and pomegranate salad

Quinoa is a nice alternative to wholemeal couscous or rice and makes an excellent backdrop for chopped vegetables, fruits, dried fruits, nuts and seeds. These salads can be pricy when you buy them on the high street, and often the dressings are highly processed. Save money and un-process your lunchtime by making them yourself. Once you get the knack for making this salad, you can experiment with what you add – it's an excellent way to use up stray veggies and fruit from your fridge.

SERVES 4

200g quinoa
30g flaked almonds, toasted
Handful of mint leaves, chopped
Handful of flat-leaf parsley, chopped
1 yellow pepper, finely diced
80g pomegranate seeds
50g sultanas
50g kalamata olives, pitted and sliced
Sea salt and black pepper

FOR THE DRESSING
4 tbsp olive oil
Juice of 1 lemon
1 tsp honey or maple syrup
½ tsp ground cinnamon
¼ tsp sea salt

1_ Rinse the quinoa in a fine-mesh sieve under cold water for a minute, swirling it around with a fork. Place the quinoa in a saucepan with 400ml water. Bring to the boil, then cover and reduce the heat to a simmer and cook for 15 minutes. Take the pan off the heat and leave it to rest for 5 minutes with the lid on. Remove the lid and drain off any excess liquid, then fluff the quinoa with a fork and set aside to cool.

2_ Prepare the dressing by adding all the ingredients to a small cup and whisking with a fork.

3_ Transfer the quinoa to a large bowl then add all the other salad ingredients. Season to taste, then pour over the dressing and combine well before serving.

- Try serving with a dollop of guacamole (see page 131) or some sliced avocado.
- You can batch-cook this salad as it will last for up to 3 days in the fridge.
- Cook extra quinoa to create a tasty crunchy topping. Spread the cooked quinoa on a non-stick baking sheet and drizzle over a little oil and add a good pinch of salt. Place in an oven preheated to 180°C/160°C fan/Gas 4 for 25 minutes until golden and crispy, stirring a few times during cooking.

Supergreen salad with fruity lime dressing

This salad is a tasty way to get your greens. In theory, frozen vegetables are processed, but this is a healthy type of processed food that is convenient, saves on your food bill and reduces food waste. This dish uses edamame beans which are easy to get hold of in your local supermarket. The dressing on this salad is super zingy, and I have been a little greedy with it, so add less if you prefer. Dress it before you go to work so the flavours have time to combine before you eat it for lunch.

SERVES 4

3 tbsp mixed seeds (sesame, sunflower, pumpkin)
1 large, sweet apple (or 2 small)
Juice of ½ lime
1 cucumber peeled, halved lengthways, deseeded and sliced
150g frozen edamame beans, defrosted
150g sugar snap peas or mangetout, trimmed and chopped
50g baby spinach leaves, chopped
Handful of lentil sprouts (optional)

FOR THE DRESSING
Juice of 1½ limes
3 tbsp olive oil
1 tbsp sesame oil
Thumb-sized piece of fresh ginger, peeled and grated
1 tbsp honey
Handful of coriander, chopped
Sea salt

1_ Preheat the oven to 180°C/160°C fan/Gas 4.
2_ Spread the seeds out on a baking sheet and toast in the oven for 5 minutes, being careful not to burn them. Once toasted, remove from the oven and set aside to cool.
3_ Grate the apple or cut into matchsticks then place in a large bowl. Squeeze in the lime juice to prevent the apple from browning.
4_ Place the remaining salad ingredients into the bowl and combine well.
5_ Prepare the dressing by adding all the ingredients to a small jar with a lid and shaking well; alternatively you can blitz them in a food processor.
6_ Pour the dressing over the salad and toss to combine.

Super Quick Meals

Courgette ribbons with olive oil, honey and feta

This Greek-inspired quick meal takes less than five minutes to prepare and is perfect for serving during the summer months when courgettes are in season. The combination of feta and honey perfectly balances salty and sweet, while the walnuts add a crunchy texture. Don't be fooled by the fact that this is mainly courgettes; this dish still makes a satisfying meal.

SERVES 2

2 large courgettes
1 tbsp lemon juice
2 sprigs of thyme, leaves picked
Small handful of walnuts
50g feta cheese
2 tbsp olive oil
1 tbsp honey
Sea salt

1_ Trim the courgette ends, then use a vegetable peeler to cut very long, thin slices of courgette to create 'ribbons'.

2_ Arrange the courgette ribbons in a serving bowl, add the lemon juice and toss gently. Add the thyme leaves and walnuts, crushing them in your hands slightly as you go. Crumble over the feta cheese.

3_ Gently warm the olive oil in a small pan with the honey then pour over the courgette.

4_ Season with salt and serve immediately.

Egg burrito with avocado and spinach

This dish was a TikTok sensation and is a very clever idea for a quick meal, as it takes less than five minutes to make. Using egg as a base means you are getting a good source of protein and B12 – particularly good for vegetarians who may struggle to get enough of these nutrients. I use the homemade Wholemeal tortillas in this recipe (see page 190), another good reason to make a batch of them and stock them in your freezer to save time. Shop-bought tortillas have an unusually long shelf life of months and a very long ingredient list to support this. This burrito is perfect in the morning for a breakfast on the go, too.

SERVES 1

1 tbsp extra virgin olive oil
3 eggs, beaten
1 Wholemeal flour tortilla (see page 190)
½ avocado, sliced
½ tomato, sliced
Handful of baby spinach
Hot sauce (see page 209) or Tomato
    ketchup (see page 199) (optional)
Sea salt and black pepper

1_ Heat the oil in a non-stick frying pan that is large enough to comfortably fit a tortilla.
2_ Pour the eggs into the pan and cook for 30 seconds, then place the tortilla on top of the egg and gently press down. Cook for 1–2 minutes more so the egg can set, then flip over.
3_ Place the sliced avocado, tomatoes and spinach on one half of the tortilla then drizzle over the sauce, season with salt and pepper and cook for a further 1 minute so the tortilla gets slightly crispy.
4_ Take the pan off the heat and fold the tortilla then cut in half and serve.
5_ Serve on its own or with salad.

Coconut soup three ways

These three soups are so simple that opening an ultra-processed tin is not even worth bothering. All three soups are creamy and vegan-friendly, using fresh coconut milk, which can be made in no time using dried coconut and water. You can make all three of these soups in batches and freeze them for up to 12 months to ensure you always have something nutritious to hand when you get caught short.

Spinach and coconut soup

SERVES 4

400ml Coconut milk (see page 203)
600g fresh spinach (you can also use frozen)
2 garlic cloves, finely chopped
Pinch of freshly grated nutmeg
Sea salt and black pepper

1_ Pour the coconut milk into a saucepan set over a medium heat.
2_ Add the spinach, garlic and nutmeg and bring to the boil. Reduce the heat and simmer gently for 5 minutes.
3_ Remove the pan from the heat and blitz with a stick blender until smooth.
4_ Season with salt and pepper, before serving with a decorative drizzle of coconut milk across the top.

Tomato and coconut soup

SERVES 4–6

400g Coconut milk (see page 203)
3 x 400g tins cherry tomatoes
3 garlic cloves, crushed
Sea salt and black pepper

1_ Pour the coconut milk and tomatoes into a saucepan set over a medium heat.
2_ Add the garlic cloves and bring to the boil. Reduce the heat and simmer gently for 5 minutes.
3_ Remove the pan from the heat and blitz with a stick blender until smooth.
4_ Season with salt and pepper, before serving with a decorative drizzle of coconut milk across the top.

Butternut squash and coconut soup

SERVES 4

1 large butternut squash, peeled, deseeded and chopped
2 garlic cloves, unpeeled and left whole
600ml Vegetable stock (see page 215) or water
400ml Coconut milk (see page 203)
½ red chilli, chopped
Sea salt and black pepper

1_ Preheat the oven to 180°C/160°C fan/Gas 4. Line a baking tray with parchment paper.
2_ Spread out the squash and garlic cloves on the baking tray and season with salt and pepper. Transfer to the oven and roast for 35 minutes until the squash is tender. Once cooked, squeeze the garlic out of the skin.
3_ Set a large saucepan over a medium-high heat and pour in the stock and coconut milk. Add the roasted squash, garlic and red chilli and bring to the boil. Reduce the heat and simmer for 5 minutes.
4_ Remove the pan from the heat and blitz with a stick blender until smooth.
5_ Check the seasoning before serving with a decorative drizzle of coconut milk across the top.

Huevos rancheros

This simple and nutritious dish is traditionally served for breakfast, but it also makes a great quick lunch or dinner option. Making your own wholemeal tortillas is a less ultra-processed option compared to pre-packaged white flour wraps – store them in batches in the freezer to save time. Add black beans to the sauce if you fancy something more filling.

SERVES 2

2 tbsp extra virgin olive oil
1 small red onion, chopped
1 green chilli, finely chopped
2 tsp mild chilli powder
400g tin chopped tomatoes
Juice of ½ lime
2 Wholemeal tortillas (see page 190)
2 large eggs
2 spring onions, thinly sliced
2 tbsp Greek yoghurt
2 tbsp chopped coriander (optional)
Sea salt and black pepper

1_ Place a saucepan over a medium heat and add 1 tablespoon of the oil. Once hot, add the onion and fry for 5 minutes until softened.

2_ Add the green chilli and chilli powder and fry for 1 minute. Add the tomatoes and lime juice and bring the sauce to the boil, then reduce the heat and simmer gently for 12 minutes. Season with salt and pepper.

3_ Set a large non-stick frying pan over a medium heat. When hot, add the tortillas one at a time and cook on each side for 1–2 minutes until softened and bubbling slightly. Remove the tortillas from the pan and wrap them in foil to keep warm.

4_ Using the same frying pan add the remaining tablespoon of oil and crack in the eggs. Cook the eggs for 3–4 minutes, or until the whites have set but the yolks are still runny.

5_ To serve, place one tortilla on each plate and spoon the sauce over, then top with a fried egg.

6_ Add a scattering of spring onions, a dollop of Greek yoghurt and the coriander (if using), and serve. Break off bits of tortilla to use as dippers.

Kashmiri prawns

These prawns are so good and use Kashmiri chilli powder, which is milder than other varieties. If you are using cayenne pepper as a replacement, then go easy as it is a lot spicier. A fail-safe way to create tasty unprocessed or minimally processed meals is to keep it super simple by adding dried spices to poultry, fish and tofu. And don't just serve these prawns for dinner – they can be batch-cooked and eaten as a high-protein snack. Try wrapping them in lettuce leaves with a drizzle of Tahini dressing (see page 207) if you have any leftovers in the fridge.

SERVES 4

300g brown rice
400g raw peeled king prawns (defrosted if frozen)
2 tsp ground turmeric
½ tsp ground coriander
½ tsp ground cumin
¼ tsp ground cardamom
3 tsp Kashmiri chilli powder or 2 tsp cayenne pepper
1 tbsp lemon juice
Thumb-sized piece of fresh ginger, half peeled and grated, half peeled and cut into matchsticks
1 tbsp extra virgin olive oil
8 curry leaves
2 green chillies, halved and deseeded
1 onion, thinly sliced
1 avocado, peeled and sliced
2 tbsp desiccated coconut
Handful of coriander, leaves picked
Sea salt and black pepper

1_ Place the rice in a sieve and rinse under cold water a few times. Bring a large saucepan of water to the boil, then add the rice, reduce the heat and simmer for 25–30 minutes until tender.

2_ Rinse the prawns under cold water, then pat dry. Put the spices, lemon juice, grated ginger and a pinch of salt into a small bowl and combine well, then add the prawns and stir with a spoon to coat before setting aside.

3_ Set a large non-stick frying pan over a medium heat and add the oil. Once hot, add the curry leaves, chilli, ginger matchsticks and sliced onion and cook for 8–10 minutes until softened and translucent. Season with black pepper.

4_ Tip the prawns and any leftover marinade into the frying pan and stir-fry for about 5 minutes until they are cooked through.

5_ Serve the prawns with brown rice and avocado slices and sprinkle with the coconut and coriander leaves.

• If you like your food with less heat, halve the amount of chilli powder or cayenne pepper.

Avocado baked eggs

This is not a new idea, but it's still a goodie, and it looks great on the plate. Eggs are obviously unprocessed, but they are also nutritional powerhouses as they contain nearly every essential vitamin and mineral required for the body to work correctly. Avocados are the perfect partner, containing high amounts of vitamin E and monounsaturated fatty acids that can help maintain healthy cholesterol levels in the blood.

SERVES 2

2 ripe avocados
4 small eggs
Pinch of paprika
Sea salt and black pepper
2 slices of Seeded wholemeal and rye loaf (see page 191)
Sliced spring onion, chopped coriander and sliced chilli, to garnish (optional)

1_ Preheat the oven to 200°C/180°C fan/Gas 6.
2_ Cut the avocados in half and remove the stones. Scoop out a small amount of the flesh to make room for the eggs.
3_ Put the avocados into a small ovenproof dish close together so they don't tip over while they are cooking.
4_ Break an egg into each avocado half and sprinkle with paprika, salt and pepper, then bake in the oven for 15 minutes, or until the egg sets.
5_ Just before your eggs are cooked, toast the seeded bread slices.
6_ Serve one whole avocado per person with a slice of toast on the side. You can also garnish these with slices of spring onion, chopped coriander and sliced chilli, if you like.

- Vegans could try filling the avocado with lightly crushed spiced chickpeas and chopped cherry tomatoes or a spicy rice mixture.
- Use Wholemeal tortillas or Wholemeal pitta breads (see pages 190 and 194) if you have batch-cooked these previously and have a stash in the freezer.

Homemade pot noodle

There is nothing pleasant about a pot noodle: hot water flavoured with monosodium glutamate (MSG) and other flavour enhancers, thickeners like guar gum and sweeteners like dried glucose syrup. You will also find a few dried peas and sweetcorn bobbing around. You can do it yourself with fresh stock, wholewheat noodles and fresh vegetables in less than 5 minutes. Tamari is just fermented soya beans and contains no MSG.

SERVES 2

300ml Chicken stock (see page 215)
120g wholemeal egg noodles
2 tbsp frozen peas
2 tbsp frozen sweetcorn
Handful of leftover shredded chicken
    (optional)
1 tbsp tamari
1 tbsp lime juice (optional)
1 large spring onion, thinly sliced
½ red chilli, thinly sliced

1_ Place the chicken stock in a saucepan set over a medium heat and bring to the boil. Add the egg noodles and turn the heat down to a gentle simmer, then add the peas, sweetcorn and chicken (if using) and cook for 4 minutes until the noodles are tender.

2_ Add the tamari and lime juice (if using), then divide between 2 bowls. Garnish with the spring onion and red chilli.

- You can also use soba noodles in this recipe but they will need to be cooked first then added to the finished broth.

Avocado pesto with wholemeal spaghetti

There seems to be no end to what you can do with an avocado, and social media continues to provide new and exciting ideas. This is not new, but it is delicious and is an excellent option for vegans (use non-dairy yoghurt in the pesto and leave out the Parmesan shavings). If you want something a bit different, try using coriander instead of basil in the pesto sauce; you can also add leftover shredded roast chicken for added protein.

SERVES 4

450g wholemeal spaghetti
1 red chilli, finely chopped
4 tbsp pine nuts, toasted
4 tbsp Parmesan shavings
Sea salt

FOR THE PESTO
2 ripe avocados, stoned and chopped
Zest and juice of 1 lemon
2 garlic cloves, chopped
Small bunch of basil or coriander
4 tbsp extra virgin olive oil
1 tbsp natural yoghurt

1_ Bring a large saucepan of water to the boil, add the spaghetti and cook for 12–14 minutes until cooked with a little bite ('al dente').

2_ Meanwhile, put the avocado, lemon zest and juice, garlic, basil (or coriander), olive oil and yoghurt into a food processor and blitz until thick and smooth. Season with a little salt.

3_ Drain the spaghetti then return to the hot pan. Add the avocado pesto and stir to combine.

4_ Serve in bowls topped with the chopped chilli, pine nuts and Parmesan shavings.

- This pesto sauce is great to use instead of butter on toast, which you can then top with shredded chicken, crumbled feta cheese or scrambled tofu.
- You can use any type of pasta in place of spaghetti, such as fusilli or penne.
- This dish looks (and tastes) great with some halved cherry tomatoes.

Potato, edamame and tuna salad with red pepper dressing

Potatoes seem to have fallen out of fashion but provide the perfect carbohydrate base to a nourishing salad. Fresh protein can be expensive and so there is an option to use tinned in this recipe; tinned tuna can be viewed as a 'healthy' processed food that solves the problem of avoiding ultra-processed food while still fitting in with the food budget. This recipe is a good way to make use of the versatile red pepper sauce if you have any left over. This dish can also be pre-prepped for a packed lunch – just remember to keep the dressing separate.

SERVES 2

300g new potatoes
150g frozen edamame beans, defrosted
150g fine green beans, trimmed
240g fresh tuna steak
Extra virgin olive oil, for drizzling
Handful of rocket leaves
3–4 tbsp Versatile roasted red pepper
    sauce (see page 200)
Sea salt and black pepper

1_ Bring a saucepan of water to the boil, add the potatoes and cook for 15 minutes until tender. Add the edamame beans and green beans and cook for a further 2 minutes. Drain the potatoes and beans then rinse under cold water for a minute so they retain their green colour. Leave to one side until the potatoes are completely cool.

2_ Now prepare the tuna. Set a large non-stick frying pan over a high heat. Rub the tuna with a little oil and season with salt and pepper. Once the pan is hot add the tuna and sear for 1–2 minutes on each side (longer if you like it cooked through). Transfer the tuna to a chopping board and leave to rest for 5 minutes, then slice into thin strips. You can serve the tuna warm or cold.

3_ Once cooled, cut the potatoes in half lengthways then transfer to a bowl with the other vegetables and the rocket. Add the tuna slices to the salad, then toss everything together lightly. Season with salt and pepper.

4_ Serve in bowls and drizzle over the red pepper sauce or serve on the side.

• You can use a tin of tuna in oil or spring water in this recipe instead of fresh.

Snacks & Puddings

Baked peaches with pistachio crumble and lime yoghurt

Fruit crumbles are high on everyone's list of favourite puddings. This crumble has been deconstructed but still has all the delicious key elements of warm fruit and crunchy oat topping. You can also make it in smaller bowls for kids and serve hot with homemade ice cream (see page 172).

SERVES 4

4 large ripe peaches, stoned and sliced
  into eighths
2 tbsp honey
150g Greek yoghurt
Zest and juice of ½ lime

FOR THE CRUMBLE
100g porridge oats
50g pistachio nuts, crushed
25g wholemeal flour
1 tbsp olive oil
2 tbsp runny honey
Pinch of ground cinnamon

1_ Preheat the oven to 180°C/160°C fan/Gas 4.
2_ Put the peach slices and honey into a bowl and combine well. Transfer the slices to a baking dish, flat side facing up.
3_ To make the crumble place all the ingredients into a bowl and mix well using your fingers.
4_ Cover the peaches with the crumble and bake in the oven for 20 minutes until the topping is golden and crisp.
5_ While the peaches are in the oven make the lime yoghurt by mixing together the yoghurt and lime zest and juice.
6_ Remove the peaches from the oven and serve in bowls with a dollop of lime yoghurt. Sprinkle any remaining crumble left in the dish over the peaches.

Frozen mango yoghurt

Have you ever wondered why manufactured ice cream and frozen yoghurt turns to a foamy slime rather than melting? This is because of the way it is manufactured and because it contains ingredients such as guar gum, locust bean gum, alginate, carrageenan and xanthan gum, all used to replace more expensive ingredients and to prolong shelf life.

SERVES 4

600g frozen mango
125g full-fat Greek yoghurt
2 tbsp honey

1_ Place the ingredients in a food processor and blitz for 4–5 minutes until completely smooth.
2_ Transfer the mixture to an airtight container and freeze for a few hours until ready to serve.

- You can try this with any frozen fruits you like.
- If you have the time, you can whisk the ice cream with a fork every half hour or so to create a creamier frozen yoghurt.

Cheat's chocolate ice cream

This banana-based ice cream is like magic and is a great pudding to prepare with your kids. It is also free from added sugars as the bananas have enough sweetness, though it works best with bananas that have started to go brown. You'll need to remember to peel the bananas and cut them into chunks before you freeze them. Once you have mastered the basic recipe, you can experiment with many other flavours.

SERVES 4

6–8 very ripe bananas (about 800g), cut into chunks and frozen
50ml milk (or dairy-free alternative)
3 tbsp unsweetened cocoa powder
2 tbsp Smooth nut butter (see page 205)

1_ Place all the ingredients in a food processor and pulse to break down the frozen bananas. Scrape down the sides of the food processor, then blitz for 1–2 minutes until completely smooth.

2_ Serve immediately or transfer to an airtight container and freeze.

- You can experiment with different flavours using fruits and spices in place of the cocoa powder and nut butter.
- If you are making this in advance you'll need to remove the ice cream from the freezer about 10 minutes before you serve, to make it soft enough to scoop.

Vegan chocolate mousse

There is no reason to miss out on a great pudding like chocolate mousse just because you choose to eat a plant-based diet. The food industry has responded to the growing interest in veganism and plant-based eating by producing a vast amount of ultra-processed foods tailored to this market. Ironically it is now almost easier to be an unhealthy vegan than a healthy one, with a lot of processing used to recreate vegan versions of food, including a variety of puddings and snacks. This recipe is a simple way to make a very healthy chocolate mousse from creamy avocados. It works best when they are very ripe.

SERVES 4

2 large ripe avocados
4 tbsp maple syrup
3 tbsp raw cacao or unsweetened
     cocoa powder
1 vanilla pod, slit lengthways and
     seeds removed
Pinch of salt

1_ Peel the avocado then remove the stone and scoop the flesh into a food processor or blender. Add the remaining ingredients and blitz until completely smooth and creamy.

2_ Divide the mousse mixture between 4 small ramekins or glasses and chill in the fridge for an hour before serving.

Orange, cardamom and honey polenta cake

Sometimes you want a nice plain bit of cake when sharing a pot of tea or coffee with a friend. This simple cake uses polenta and ground almonds, making it gluten-free. Shop-bought cakes are laden with ultra-processed ingredients, which is why they have such a long shelf life. This cake couldn't be easier to make as you just add the wet ingredients to the dry, stir and bake for 20 minutes.

SERVES 6

100g fine polenta
200g ground almonds
Zest and juice of 2 oranges
200ml olive oil
160g honey
4 eggs
2 tbsp flaked almonds, toasted

FOR THE GLAZE
Juice of 2 oranges
Crushed seeds from 6 cardamom pods or
 1 tsp ground cardamom
50ml honey

1_ Preheat the oven to 180°C/160°C fan/Gas 4. Line a 20cm cake tin with parchment paper.

2_ Put the polenta, almonds and orange zest in a large bowl and combine well.

3_ Put the orange juice, olive oil, honey and eggs into another bowl and whisk together.

4_ Pour the wet mixture into the bowl with the dry ingredients and stir together until they are completely combined.

5_ Transfer the batter to the lined cake tin and bake in the oven for 20–25 minutes. You can test if the cake is cooked by inserting a skewer, which should come back out clean.

6_ While the cake is in the oven, make the glaze by combining the orange juice, cardamom and honey in a small bowl and whisking together.

7_ Take the cake out of the oven and pierce the top all over with a skewer. Pour over the glaze, then scatter with the flaked almonds. Leave in the tin for 5 minutes to cool.

8_ Remove the cake from the tin and transfer to a wire rack to cool completely before serving.

• Don't be alarmed if it sinks slightly after baking – this can happen when there is no gluten to maintain the structure.

Coconut rice pudding with fresh mango and lime coulis

Unctuous is the only way to describe this delicious rice pudding, which is creamy, moreish and naturally sweet with the flavour of fresh coconut milk. Rice pudding is a straightforward dessert to prepare, and it works wonderfully well with the aromatic and citrus fruitiness of mango and lime, which helps to cut through the sweetness. Homemade rice pudding also tastes so much better than anything you'll get out of a tin.

SERVES 4

150g pudding rice
400ml Coconut milk (see page 203)
250ml whole milk (or a plant-based
    alternative – see page 214)
3 tbsp honey
1 tsp ground cinnamon
1 large ripe mango
Juice of ½ small lime
2 tbsp desiccated coconut or coconut
    flakes

1_ Put the rice, both milks, honey and cinnamon into a saucepan and bring to the boil. Reduce the heat and simmer for 20–25 minutes until the rice is cooked and the liquid has been absorbed. Stir occasionally to prevent the rice from sticking to the bottom of the pan.

2_ Remove half the flesh from the mango and place in a blender with a squeeze of lime. Cut the remaining mango flesh into small cubes. Put both the mango purée and the cubes into a bowl and mix together.

3_ Serve the rice pudding in small bowls topped with the mango and a sprinkle of coconut.

- You can use frozen mango if you like but defrost before using and cut into smaller pieces.
- You can also use lychees instead of mango.
- Vegans can replace the honey with maple syrup.

Snacks & Puddings

High-protein energy bars

Energy and protein bars have become a big business, but the formulations are far from natural. As a rule of thumb, if a snack food has several health claims, it will likely be ultra-processed – the irony. They generally use a sweetener (polyols, which can have a laxative effect if you overeat them) to be classed as 'low sugar', various protein powders, bovine collagen for chewiness and something to add fibre, like polydextrose, made in a lab and not digested in the body. This homemade version is going to be different. However, it will still give you 12g of protein per bar and a host of other vital nutrients.

MAKES 8

480g dried chickpeas, soaked and cooked
    (see page 64)
10 soft dates, pitted
4 tbsp honey
8 tbsp crunchy peanut or almond butter
    (see page 205)
75g ground almonds
½ tsp baking powder
150g mixed seeds (sunflower, linseed,
    sesame)
100ml milk or Oat or Coconut milk
    (see pages 214 and 203)

1_ Preheat the oven to 180°C/160°C fan/Gas 4. Line a 20cm square cake tin with parchment paper.
2_ Tip the chickpeas into a food processor, add the dates, honey and nut butter and blitz into a smooth paste. Add the remaining ingredients, then blitz again until smooth.
3_ Transfer the mixture to the cake tin then spread out and smooth with a spatula.
4_ Place the tin in the oven and bake for 25 minutes, or until a knife inserted into the mixture comes out clean.
5_ Leave to cool in the pan for 10 minutes, then tip out of the pan onto a board. Cut into 8 pieces.

- You can store these bars in an airtight container for up to 5 days, or they can be frozen for up to 3 months.
- You can use 2 x 400g cans of chickpeas (rinsed and drained).
- These energy bars can be made with cocoa powder by adding 3 tbsp in step 2.

Oat and sultana cookies

These simple cookies score so much better on the processed food scale than ultra-processed shop-bought cookies as making them yourself means you control what goes into them. Oats are a whole, unprocessed food, and these cookies are sweetened with honey over white sugar, which is a more natural sweetener. This is a lovely recipe to use any homemade nut butter you have made, which can also be made in batches and even frozen.

MAKES 12

125g whole rolled oats
½ tsp bicarbonate of soda
1 tsp ground cinnamon
125g Smooth nut butter (peanut, cashew or almond – see page 205)
75g honey
1 egg, beaten
4 tbsp sultanas, chopped

1_ Preheat the oven to 170°C/150°C fan/Gas 3. Line 2 baking trays with parchment paper.

2_ Put the oats into a food processor and blitz to about half their size, then add the bicarbonate of soda and cinnamon and pulse a few times to combine. Transfer to a large bowl.

3_ Put the nut butter, honey and egg in a separate bowl and whisk to combine, then pour this into the oat mixture with the sultanas and mix until completely combined.

4_ Take one tablespoon of the mixture per biscuit and roll into a ball (wet hands helps with this) then arrange on the baking trays leaving a 2cm gap between each one. Flatten the cookies to about 1cm thick.

5_ Place the cookies in the oven and bake for 12–14 minutes until golden brown. Leave the cookies to cool on the tray before eating or storing in an airtight container.

Coconut and vanilla macaroons

I love these chewy little bites; they are perfect to satisfy a sweet tooth with a nice cup of tea or coffee when you're sitting at your desk working. This recipe replaces white sugar with honey and uses less of it, as the coconut has plenty of natural sweetness. Vanilla extract gives you a natural hit of vanilla, rather than essence, which is a synthetic version. Shop-bought versions of these macaroons are often dipped in chocolate and sweetened with glucose syrup made from the hydrolysis of starch.

MAKES ABOUT 12

2 large egg whites
4 tbsp light coloured honey
200g desiccated coconut
1 tsp vanilla extract
Sea salt

1_ Place the egg whites and honey in a large clean bowl and whisk for 2 minutes until light and frothy. Add the coconut, vanilla and a pinch of salt, then stir to combine well. Leave to sit for 10 minutes to soften up the coconut.

2_ Preheat the oven to 170°C/150°C fan/Gas 3 and line a baking sheet with parchment paper.

3_ Use a tablespoon to scoop out the mixture, then roll and squeeze into 12 compact balls. Arrange them on the baking sheet, then transfer to the oven and bake for 12–14 minutes until golden.

4_ Leave to cool completely before storing.

- These macaroons will keep for about 3 days in an airtight container.
- Explore different varieties of honey as they will give you different tastes.

Walnut and banana bread

Everyone loves a bit of cake, and sometimes you just want something simple, tasty and plain, which you can get from a good loaf cake. This one is made using wholemeal flour and honey instead of sugar. It has a muffin-like texture, staying moist for a few days when stored in an airtight container. Shop-bought cakes contain all manner of ultra-processed ingredients to help prolong their shelf life, including the preservative potassium sorbate and the stabilizer xanthan gum.

MAKES ONE 900G LOAF
(12 SLICES)

75ml light olive oil
120g honey
2 eggs
2 very ripe bananas, peeled and mashed
4 tbsp milk
1 tsp bicarbonate of soda
1 tsp ground cinnamon, plus extra
   for dusting
½ tsp freshly grated nutmeg
225g wholemeal flour
4 tbsp chopped walnuts

1_ Preheat the oven to 160°C/140°C fan/Gas 2. Line a 900g loaf tin with parchment paper.

2_ Whisk together the olive oil and honey in a large bowl. Add the eggs, mashed bananas and milk and beat well to combine, then add the bicarbonate of soda and spices and whisk again. Using a spatula, fold the flour and walnuts into the wet ingredients.

3_ Pour the batter into the prepared loaf tin and sprinkle the top with a little cinnamon. Place the loaf tin in the oven and bake for 50–55 minutes, or until a knife inserted into the centre of the loaf comes out clean.

4_ Remove the banana loaf from the oven and leave to cool in the tin for 10 minutes before transferring to a wire rack to cool completely.

- You can freeze this cake for up to 3 months by wrapping tightly in cling film.
- Try topping with Smooth nut butter (see page 205). You can also make a much thicker nut milk with the consistency of cream to spread on the bread – try using cashew nuts.

Sweet potato brownies

There is something very moreish about a good squidgy chocolate brownie.
Still, if you read the ingredient lists of some shop-bought varieties, it can be
off-putting. Often ingredients will include modified starches, inverted sugar
syrups, preservatives and emulsifiers, which are added to help maintain
texture, taste and shelf life. These brownies are as unprocessed as you can
get, with natural sweetness and gooey texture provided by the sweet potato
and dates, which also give a valuable dose of crucial nutrients, including the
antioxidant beta-carotene.

MAKES 9

600g sweet potatoes, peeled and diced
   into 1cm cubes
225g Medjool dates, pitted
80g ground almonds
100g plain wholemeal flour
4 tbsp unsweetened cocoa powder
4 tbsp honey
Pinch of sea salt
1 tbsp Smooth nut butter (see page 205),
   made with almonds

1_ Preheat the oven to 180°C/160°C fan/Gas 4. Line the base
    and sides of a 20cm square cake tin with parchment paper.
2_ Wrap the sweet potato chunks in foil and place on a baking
    tray then bake in the oven for 20 minutes, or until soft.
3_ Once the sweet potato is cooked, remove from the oven
    and leave to cool slightly before transferring to a food
    processor along with the dates. Blitz to form a smooth
    paste.
4_ Transfer the paste to a large bowl and add the remaining
    ingredients (except the almond butter) and stir to
    combine well.
5_ Add the mixture to the lined cake tin then drizzle the
    almond butter over the batter and swirl with a knife. Place
    the tin in the oven to bake for 15–20 minutes. You can test
    if they are cooked by piercing with a knife – if it comes out
    with just a few crumbs attached it is ready (it is better to
    undercook these than risk them drying out too much).
6_ Once cooked, remove the brownies from the oven and leave
    to cool completely in the tin before removing and slicing
    into 9 squares.

•   These brownies will last for up
    to 5 days stored in an airtight
    container in the fridge – or you can
    freeze them for up to 3 months.

Bombay mix

Bombay mix is a tasty, savoury snack made from dried nuts, lentils and spices. You can make your own using Indian-spiced roasted chickpeas as a base, with coconuts, raisins and nuts to give a lovely salty-sweet taste sensation. The key to this dish is a really crunchy roasted chickpea, so make sure they are bone dry before they go in the oven. This snack is also a great way to boost your fibre intake.

SERVES 4–6

480g dried chickpeas, soaked and
    cooked (see page 64)
1 tsp extra virgin olive oil
1 tsp caraway seeds
1 tbsp medium curry powder
4 tbsp unsalted peanuts
2 tbsp desiccated coconut
2 tbsp curry leaves (optional)
2 tbsp raisins or golden sultanas
Sea salt

1_ Preheat the oven to 200°C/180°C fan/Gas 6. Line a baking tray with parchment paper.

2_ Tip the drained chickpeas onto a clean tea towel and rub dry to remove as much moisture as possible – the drier your chickpea the crunchier it will become when you roast it. The skins will come loose, and this will help with the end 'crunch'.

3_ Transfer the chickpeas to a large bowl, removing and discarding the skins. This is slightly cumbersome, but you will get a better end result. Add the oil and toss well, then add the caraway seeds, curry powder and a pinch of salt and toss well to fully coat the chickpeas.

4_ Tip the chickpeas onto the baking tray and place in the oven to cook for 15 minutes. Remove the tray from the oven, add the peanuts and roast for a further 7 minutes. Remove the tray one more time and add the coconut and curry leaves, then roast again for a final 5 minutes.

5_ Remove the tray from the oven and leave to cool. If your chickpeas are not completely dry when you start to roast them then it may take longer to cook, so add an extra 5 minutes, taking care not to burn the nuts and coconut.

6_ Allow the mixture to cool completely then tip into a bowl and add the raisins and a little salt before combining well.

• You can use 2 x 400g tins chickpeas in this recipe (rinsed and drained) instead of dried.
• This mix will keep for a few days in an airtight container like a Mason jar.

Roasted carrot hummus

Everyone loves hummus; it makes an excellent snack for children and if you serve it with cucumber and red pepper slices, will encourage them to eat more vegetables. Homemade hummus tastes fresher than something manufactured but will only last for a short time because it won't contain preservatives. You can experiment with different flavours, such as using the same weight of beetroot or red pepper instead of carrots.

SERVES 6

8 carrots, peeled and cut into small chunks (about 800g)
2 garlic cloves, unpeeled
5 tbsp extra virgin olive oil
½ tsp ground cumin
2 tbsp light tahini
Juice of ½ lemon
50g dried chickpeas, soaked and cooked (see page 64)
Sea salt

1_ Preheat the oven to 200°C/180°C fan/Gas 6.
2_ Place the carrots and garlic on a baking sheet and drizzle with 1 tablespoon of the oil. Sprinkle over the cumin and season with a little salt then roast in the oven for 30 minutes, or until tender. Once cooked remove from the oven and set aside to cool. Squeeze the garlic cloves out of their skins.
3_ Transfer the carrots and garlic to a food processor or blender and add the remaining 4 tablespoons of olive oil, the tahini, lemon juice, chickpeas and ½ teaspoon salt. Add 4 tablespoons of water and blitz until smooth, adding more water if needed to loosen the mixture. Taste and adjust the seasoning.
4_ Serve the hummus with sliced Wholemeal pitta breads (see page 194) and vegetable crudites.

- This hummus will keep in the fridge for up to 5 days and you can freeze it for up to 4 months.
- You can use 1 x 215g tin chickpeas (rinsed and drained) for this recipe instead of dried.

Vegetable crisps

Vegetable crisps give a lot more natural flavour than artificially flavoured potato crisps and you can make them yourself for a fraction of the cost. The key to an excellent homemade crisp is to dry the vegetables really well before you bake them and make sure they are sliced as thinly as possible using a peeler or mandoline – mind your fingers. If you want to spice them up a little, add chilli powder, ground cumin or smoked paprika.

SERVES 4–6

2 carrots, very thinly sliced
1 large raw parsnip, very thinly sliced
2 raw beetroots, very thinly sliced
1 tbsp olive oil
Sea salt

1_ Preheat the oven to 190°C/170°C fan/Gas 5.
2_ Lay out the sliced vegetables on sheets of kitchen paper and pat them dry (the drier they are the crisper they will become when roasted), then transfer to a large bowl. Drizzle the oil over the vegetables, season with a little salt and toss well.
3_ Transfer the vegetables to 1 or 2 non-stick baking trays and spread them out evenly so they are not overlapping. Place the trays in the oven and bake for 15 minutes. Turn the vegetables over and cook for a further 10 minutes until golden brown and crisp.

• You can store these crisps in an airtight container for up to 3 days, but they are at their best the day you make them.

Bread

Wholemeal tortilla

These flour wraps are so versatile: use them to wrap your favourite fillings, for Mexican-themed nights with the family, toasted to serve with dips such as guacamole or hummus or to make a quick and easy Egg burrito (see page 154). The ingredients are simply wholemeal flour, water and salt and a little oil, and they are easier to make than you might think. Shop-bought tortilla wraps can last for weeks in their packaging, so it goes without saying that many more ingredients are used to extend the shelf life.

MAKES 6

200g wholemeal flour, plus extra
    for dusting
120ml tepid water
1 tbsp extra virgin olive oil
Pinch of sea salt

1_ Place the flour in a bowl with the water, olive oil and salt, then knead to bring the mixture together.

2_ Transfer the dough to a lightly floured work surface and knead for 5 minutes until you have a soft, smooth ball of dough. Cover the dough with a clean tea towel and leave to rest for 1 hour.

3_ Divide the mixture into 6 pieces. Roll each piece of dough as thinly as you can to make a round shape about 20cm wide. Roll the dough then turn it by 45 degrees and roll again –continue to do this to get a nice circle shape. This might take a bit of practice at first so don't worry if you don't get a perfect circle first time.

4_ Place a large non-stick frying pan over a medium heat. Place one tortilla in the pan and cook for 1 minute on each side for a soft tortilla, or 2 minutes for a crispier tortilla to use with dips.

5_ Wrap the tortillas in foil to keep warm while you continue cooking the rest.

•   The tortillas can be kept for 2 days wrapped in cling film or frozen for up to 3 months. Transfer to the fridge to defrost or use the defrost setting on the microwave for 30 seconds or so.

Seeded wholemeal and rye loaf

Making bread is not everyone's cup of tea, but I urge you to try it. Once I'd learned how to make this loaf and discovered how tasty it was, I never went back to shop-bought bread. The basics of bread are flour, yeast and salt, and you can buy a decent loaf made this way from a good bakery. However, ultra-processed packaged varieties contain more than four times the number of ingredients, including emulsifiers and preservatives to lengthen shelf life. I would recommend making two loaves at a time and freezing one.

MAKES 1 LOAF (12 SLICES)

400g strong wholemeal bread flour, plus extra for dusting

100g rye flour

7g sachet fast-action dried yeast

1 tsp finely ground sea salt

1 tbsp honey

250ml tepid water

Extra virgin olive oil, for greasing

5 tbsp mixed pumpkin and sunflower seeds

1 egg yolk, beaten

• You can freeze this bread for up to 6 months. A good tip is to slice the bread before you freeze it as frozen bread can be popped straight into the toaster.

1_ Place the flours, yeast and salt in a bowl and stir to combine. Place the honey and tepid water in a jug and mix well. Stir the liquid into the flour to make a slightly sticky dough. Add a little more water if you need to, a tablespoon at a time.

2_ Transfer the dough to a lightly floured work surface and knead for 10 minutes (or in a stand mixer fitted with the dough hook for 5–7 minutes). The dough should be smooth and elastic when it's ready. Lightly oil a bowl using kitchen paper then transfer the dough to the bowl, flipping it over to coat in the oil. Cover the bowl with cling film and leave in a warm place for 1 hour, or until the dough has doubled in size. Lightly oil a 900g loaf tin.

3_ Once the dough has doubled in size, knead again for 3–5 minutes. Add 3 tablespoons of the seeds and work them into the dough as you knead.

4_ Shape the dough to roughly the same shape as the tin then place it in the tin. Cover the tin with cling film and leave to prove for 30–45 minutes until the dough has doubled in size again. Preheat the oven to 200°C/180°C fan/Gas 6.

5_ Check the dough has had enough time to prove by pressing your finger into the loaf. If the dough springs back straight away, then it is not ready. If your finger indentation doesn't move, then it is ready to bake. Glaze the loaf with the egg yolk and sprinkle over the remaining seeds. Bake in the oven for 40–45 minutes until golden brown (the bottom of the loaf should sound hollow when tapped).

6_ Remove the loaf from the tin and leave to cool on a wire rack before slicing.

Wholemeal pitta breads

Pitta breads are a versatile addition to your bread bin as they can be filled with anything or served with dips. These pitta breads use just four ingredients and are simple to make as no proving is involved, unlike other types of bread. Shop-bought pitta bread can contain many ingredients, including emulsifiers, preservatives, flour treatment agents, dextrose and stabilizers such as xanthan gum.

MAKES 6

120g wholemeal flour
1½ tsp baking powder
¼ tsp sea salt
180g full-fat Greek yoghurt

1_ Place the flour, baking powder and salt in a bowl and combine with your hands.
2_ Add the yoghurt to the flour in three parts, mixing with your hands each time until the dough is smooth.
3_ Wrap the dough in cling film and let it rest at room temperature for an hour.
4_ Divide the dough into 6 portions and roll each one into a ball. Using a rolling pin, flatten each ball into an oval shape about 15cm in diameter.
5_ Heat a large non-stick frying pan over a medium-high heat. Transfer one piece of dough to the pan and cook for 1–2 minutes on each side, flipping when you start to see the dough puff up. Remove the pitta bread from the pan and set aside to cool.
6_ Repeat with the remaining pieces of dough.

- Substitute double cream for yoghurt or crème fraîche for a lighter sauce.
- To freeze the pitta breads, leave them to cool, wrap in cling film and store in the freezer for up to 3 months. Frozen pitta bread can be placed straight into the toaster.

Wholemeal rolls

Making your own rolls feels very self-sufficient, especially when you make them in a batch, as you'll always have something to hand in the freezer when needed. Shop-bought varieties of rolls require different types of emulsifiers to help improve the texture and prevent ingredients from splitting and settling, giving them a longer shelf life.

MAKES 8 LARGE OR
12 SMALL ROLLS

400g strong wholemeal bread flour, plus
    extra for dusting
100g strong white bread flour
7g sachet fast-action dried yeast
2 tsp finely ground sea salt
3 tbsp extra virgin olive oil, plus extra
    for greasing
1 tbsp honey
300ml tepid water

1_ Place the dry ingredients into a large bowl and mix with a spatula to combine well.

2_ Add the olive oil and honey to the water and mix. Make a well in the middle of the flour and add the water, then mix with the spatula to create a dough. Now use your hands to create a soft dough in the bowl – there should be nothing left on the sides of the bowl. Add a little more water if needed. The dough should be slightly sticky.

3_ Lightly flour a flat work surface and knead the dough for 10 minutes. Lightly grease a clean bowl, place the dough inside and cover with a clean tea towel. Leave to prove for about 1 hour, or until the dough has doubled in size.

4_ Knock the air out of the dough by kneading five times in the bowl. Divide the dough into 4 and split each piece again so you have 8 equal pieces. Roll each piece into a ball shape and place on a baking sheet lined with parchment paper. Leave for a further hour, or until the rolls have doubled in size.

5_ Preheat the oven to 200°C/180°C fan/Gas 6.

6_ Once risen, sprinkle the rolls with a little flour and bake in the top of the oven for about 20 minutes until golden brown. Leave to cool on a wire rack before serving.

• You can freeze these rolls for 3 months.
• For seeded rolls, add 4 tablespoons seeds to the dough before you begin kneading. Once the buns have proven, brush with beaten egg and sprinkle with 2 tablespoons of seeds before baking.

Sauces, Dressings & Milks

Tomato ketchup

Aside from the obvious tomatoes, the key ingredients in ketchup are vinegar, sugar and spices like cloves and allspice. This is simple to replicate at home, and you get much richer-tasting ketchup, not at all like the bright-red Tommy K you buy from the shop. I highly recommend you try making this yourself.

MAKES ENOUGH TO FILL A 500ML BOTTLE

2 onions, chopped
2kg plum tomatoes, chopped
2 garlic cloves, chopped
2 tbsp tomato purée
100ml water
150ml apple cider vinegar
4 tsp ground allspice
1 bay leaf
4 tsp honey
Pinch of sea salt

1_ Put the onions, tomatoes, garlic, tomato purée, water and a good pinch of salt into a large saucepan set over a medium heat. Cook for 45 minutes until the mixture has reduced to a pulp, stirring occasionally.

2_ While the tomatoes are cooking, pour the vinegar into a small saucepan with the allspice and bay leaf. Simmer over a low heat for 10 minutes, then take off the heat and set to one side.

3_ Blitz the tomato mixture with a stick blender until smooth then strain through a fine-mesh sieve into a clean pan, leaving the tomato skins and seeds behind. Press the back of spoon around the sieve to help push through as much of the mixture as possible.

4_ Pour the vinegar mixture into the pan with the tomatoes and remove the bay leaf, then add the honey and a pinch of salt. Set the pan over a medium heat and cook until the sauce has reduced to a thick, ketchup consistency.

5_ Pour the mixture through a funnel into a sterilized bottle or jar. Seal and cool completely before storing in the fridge.

• Homemade ketchup will last for about 3 weeks in the fridge in a sterilized jar, or you can freeze it in a sealed (not glass) container for up to 6 months.

Versatile roasted red pepper sauce

Everyone needs a reliable, versatile sauce when eating an unprocessed diet. This red pepper sauce can be adapted in many ways, and you will see it pop up throughout the book. It's a great way to add vitamin C to your diet, as red peppers are the richest dietary source.

MAKES ABOUT 300G

4 large red peppers
2 garlic cloves, left whole and unpeeled
½ small red onion, halved
Juice of ½ lemon
1 tsp honey or maple syrup
Sea salt

1_ Preheat the oven to 200°C/180°C fan/Gas 6.
2_ Cut the peppers in half and remove the core and seeds. Place the pepper halves on a baking sheet with the garlic and red onion and roast in the oven for 45 minutes until the skins are charred.
3_ Remove the cooked peppers from the oven and place in a large plastic bag then leave them to cool for 5 minutes. Once cool, remove the skins by rubbing gently with your fingers.
4_ Transfer the red peppers to a food processor. Squeeze the flesh out of the garlic and add to the food processor along with the onion halves, lemon juice, honey and a pinch of salt, then blitz until smooth.
5_ You can serve the sauce straight away or store in an airtight container in the fridge for a week.

Tomato sauce

Everybody should know how to make a basic tomato sauce, one which can be cooked in big batches. You can use this sauce in so many ways – as a base for pizza or pasta sauce, and in soups or stews. Even the most basic shop-bought tomato sauce will usually contain modified starches, making them an ultra-processed food.

SERVES 4

3 tbsp extra virgin olive oil
2 onions, finely chopped
3 garlic cloves, finely chopped
2kg fresh tomatoes, chopped
Small handful of basil leaves (optional)
Sea salt and black pepper

1_ Set a large saucepan over a medium heat and add the oil. Once hot, add the onions and cook gently for 5 minutes until softened. Add the garlic and fry for a further 2 minutes.
2_ Add the tomatoes and season with a good pinch of salt and pepper. Stir the mixture and then turn the heat down to very low. Let the tomatoes simmer gently for 1½ hours until the mixture has reduced to a thick consistency. Add the basil leaves (if using) and then use a stick blender to blitz the mixture to a smooth consistency.
3_ You can use the sauce immediately or leave to cool and store in an airtight container in the fridge until ready to use.

- This sauce can be frozen for up to 6 months in an airtight container.
- You can adapt this sauce in many different ways, adding herbs and spices, or chilli, or mascarpone cheese. You can also blitz roasted vegetables like peppers, carrots, courgette and aubergines through it as a way of getting your kids to get their 5-a-day. This is also a good way to use up leftover vegetables from dishes like the traybakes on pages 113 and 121.
- Adaptation ideas include: Add 1 red chilli, a handful of coriander and the juice of ½ lime. Add 2 teaspoons of smoked paprika. Add 1 teaspoon of chilli powder and the juice of ½ lime. Add 1 x 227g tin chopped tomatoes and 1 tablespoon tomato purée (this is the best for a pasta sauce).

Sauces, Dressings & Milks

Coconut milk

To be honest I didn't think this would work, and it took many attempts to try and get a regular tin-sized amount of coconut milk. Shop-bought coconut milk often uses thickeners and preservatives and when you make it yourself you get much fresher and lighter milk. You can either drink this as a milk alternative or cook with it. Making your own coconut milk means it won't contain stabilizers such as polysorbate 60 and sodium carboxymethylcellulose, which is not easy to say!

MAKES ABOUT 400ML

200g unsweetened desiccated coconut

1_ Put the coconut and 600ml water into a high-speed blender or food processor and blitz for 1–2 minutes until the coconut is well combined. It will look mushy and like you won't get any liquid out of it, but don't be tempted to add more water.

2_ Place a sieve over a large bowl, line it with a piece of muslin or a clean tea towel and pour in the milk to strain through, squeezing the cloth to get all the liquid out. It doesn't matter if some of the coconut gets into the milk if you are using it for a curry, although if you want a drinking consistency you may want to strain it again before using.

3_ Transfer to a sealed container until needed.

- Homemade coconut milk will keep in the fridge for about 5 days, although you will need to shake it well before using as it separates when chilled.
- A batch of this milk can be combined with 1 tablespoon honey and 2–3 tablespoons unsweetened cocoa powder (blitzed in a blender) to create a Bounty-flavoured milkshake.
- You can freeze coconut milk in an airtight container for up to 3 months.

Smooth nut butter

It is really quite straightforward to make your own nut butter. You can use any variety of nuts (cashew is also delicious) and the difference in taste from a shop-bought jar is significant. All you need for good nut butter is roasted nuts and a good food processor. Look at the label on any quality brand and you'll see that nuts and maybe a little salt are the only ingredients, while cheaper brands tend to add palm oil and sugar to their nut butters.

MAKES 450G

450g raw unsalted almonds, skin on, or cashew nuts or peanuts (skinless)
¼ tsp ground cinnamon (optional)
¼ tsp sea salt (optional)
Light olive oil (optional)

1_ Preheat the oven to 190°C/170°C fan/Gas 5.
2_ Spread the nuts out on a baking tray and roast for 10 minutes, shaking halfway through. Remove from the oven and allow the nuts to cool until you can comfortably handle them.
3_ Tip the nuts into a food processor or high-speed blender with the cinnamon and salt (if using), then blitz for 8 minutes, stopping regularly to scrape the sides down. The nut butter should be smooth and shiny. Add a little light olive oil to alter the consistency of the nut butter as required.
4_ Transfer to an airtight container – I use a sterilized mason jar.

- For a crunchy version reserve a quarter of the nuts. Blitz them to a course texture and set aside then stir into the finished nut butter.
- Homemade nut butters can be stored in the fridge for up to 2 weeks and you can freeze in an airtight container (not glass) for up to 6 months.
- Nuts can be expensive, but you can order them in bulk online; health food shops often have multi-buy offers too.
- Homemade nut butter is used in several recipes. You can use shop-bought as long as it is minimally processed (see page 22).

Mayonnaise

If you are living an unprocessed life, making common shop-bought alternatives like mayonnaise is well worth trying as making it yourself means you can choose good-quality ingredients. Avoid using extra virgin olive oil, however, as it can have an overpowering peppery taste that can leave your mayo tasting bitter.

SERVES 4–6

2 egg yolks
1 tsp Dijon mustard
250ml extra virgin olive oil
2 tbsp lemon juice
Sea salt

1_ Put the egg yolks and mustard in a bowl and season with a little salt, then whisk together until combined.
2_ Whisking continuously, adding a drop of oil at a time until the egg yolk and oil start to thicken.
3_ Once the egg yolk and oil are starting to come together then you can start adding more oil in a steady stream. Be patient as adding too much oil at once will cause the mayonnaise to split.
4_ Once you have a thick mayonnaise, whisk in the lemon juice.

• This mayonnaise will keep for 2 days in the fridge.

Vegan avonnaise

I love this take on 'mayonnaise', as it's a great nutritious alternative for vegans. You can add fresh herbs to this mayonnaise to flavour it differently, and it also works well as a dip. Avocados are a heart-protective food rich in healthy fats and potassium, which helps to regulate blood pressure in the body.

SERVES 4

2 avocados
2 tsp light olive oil
Juice of ½ small lemon
¼ tsp sea salt

1_ Place all the ingredients in a food processor or blender and blitz for 2 minutes until you have the consistency of mayonnaise.
2_ Serve immediately or transfer to a small airtight container and store in the fridge for 2 days.

• Try adding fresh basil leaves for a Mediterranean twist.

Tahini dressing

This dressing is so good and hugely versatile, which is why it is used in several recipes throughout this book. The best tahini is light and runny; I use a brand called Al Nakhil as it works so well in dressings.

SERVES 4

4 tbsp runny tahini paste
4 tbsp light olive oil
Juice of 1 small lemon
1 tsp honey or maple syrup
½ garlic clove, grated
6 tbsp warm water
Sea salt

1_ Place all the ingredients except the water in a small bowl and whisk to combine. Taste the dressing as sometimes lemons are super sour, so you may want to add another teaspoon of honey to balance the flavours.
2_ Gradually add the water while whisking until the mixture becomes smoother. (You can also add all the ingredients to a food processor and blitz until smooth.)
3_ Taste and season with a little salt.

• This dressing will last for up to 5 days in the fridge and 3 months in the freezer stored in an airtight container.

Everyday dressing

This dressing can be used on anything – hence the name 'everyday' dressing. The key to a decent dressing is getting the balance of sour, salty and sweet, and this dressing does just that. Try adding a tablespoon of grated fresh ginger for something a little more spicy.

SERVES 4

4 tbsp light olive oil
2 tbsp lemon juice (juice of 1 small lemon)
1 tsp honey
Pinch of sea salt

1_ Place all the ingredients in a small container with a lid (like a jam jar), then shake well to combine.

• This dressing will last for up to 3 days in the fridge in an airtight container.

Pesto sauce

Pesto is a convenient sauce to have to hand when preparing a meal in a hurry. You can stir this sauce into pasta, rice and couscous or use it as a dressing for poultry, fish and halloumi. I haven't used Parmesan cheese in this recipe, so it is vegan-friendly, and you'll barely notice the difference in taste as basil is really the hero ingredient.

SERVES 4

75g pine nuts, toasted
Juice of ½ lemon
1 garlic clove
60g basil leaves
¼ tsp sea salt
60ml extra virgin olive oil

1_ Put all the ingredients except the olive oil into a food processor and blitz until well combined.
2_ Blitz the mixture again, this time drizzling in the olive oil until the mixture turns to a smooth paste. You can add more oil to make the mixture smoother.

• This pesto will keep in the fridge for up to 5 days or in the freezer for up to 3 months in an airtight sealable container. You can also freeze pesto in ice-cube trays; just pop out into resealable freezer bags once frozen. These are great for single use, helping reduce food waste.

Hot sauce

Hot sauces like sriracha have become a common household food item. Commonly bought sauces contain many E numbers, in the form of flavour enhancers, stabilizers, acidity regulators and preservatives. Instead, you can make your own from all-natural ingredients. Experiment with the flavour and heat using different chillies.

MAKES ABOUT 200ML

75g red chillies, stalks removed and chopped
1 onion, chopped
2 garlic cloves, chopped
1 tbsp light olive oil
50ml honey
200g ripe baby plum tomatoes, chopped
75ml apple cider vinegar
Sea salt

1_ Place the chillies, onion and garlic in a food processor and blitz until almost smooth.
2_ Heat the oil in a saucepan over a medium heat and add the chilli paste. Gently fry the paste for 8 minutes, stirring frequently to soften, taking care not to burn it.
3_ Add the honey, tomatoes and vinegar and simmer for 15 minutes until the sauce has thickened slightly (it should be runny). Check for seasoning and add a little salt.
4_ Strain the mixture through a sieve into a pouring jug, then transfer to a sterilized glass bottle.

• The sauce will keep for up to 3 months stored in the fridge, or 1 year in the freezer when stored in an airtight container (not glass).

Raspberry vinaigrette

You can really taste the difference when you make a fruit dressing from scratch using real berries. Shop-bought dressings invariably rely on fruit purées, juices and stabilizers like xanthan gum to improve the texture, consistency and shelf life of the product.

SERVES 4

100g frozen raspberries
60ml light olive oil
25ml red wine vinegar
¼ small red onion, finely chopped
1 tsp honey
¼ tsp salt

1_　Put all the ingredients into a food processor or blender and blitz until smooth.

- If you are using frozen berries, then you may need to add a little honey.
- This dressing will keep in the fridge for up to 3 days, or you can freeze in an airtight container for up to 3 months.

Sweet potato and miso dressing

This sweet and zingy Asian-style dressing goes well on salads, or you can use it as a marinade or dip for chicken, shellfish or tofu. Miso delivers a savoury flavour and is a source of beneficial microorganisms that support your gut microbiota.

SERVES 6

100g sweet potato, peeled and cut into small dice
Thumb-sized piece of fresh ginger, peeled and finely chopped
2 tbsp lemon juice
2 tbsp rice wine vinegar
2½ tbsp sweet white miso
2 tsp sesame oil
75ml light olive oil
1–2 tsp tamari

1_　Preheat the oven to 200°C/180°C fan/ Gas 6.
2_　Place the sweet potato dice on a baking tray and cook in the oven for 20 minutes, or until tender. Remove from the oven and leave to cool.
3_　Once the sweet potato has cooled, add all the ingredients to a small blender and whizz until smooth. Taste and adjust the seasoning, adding more lemon juice, vinegar or tamari as needed.

- This dressing can be kept for up to 1 week in an airtight container in the fridge.

Sauces, Dressings & Milks

Nut milk

Making your own nut milk is one of those very satisfying things to do, and it tastes so much better than the pasteurized versions you buy in the supermarket. Shop-bought nut milks also contain several gums to stabilize the product, which you don't need when making your own. It's also cheaper to make your own, so I urge you to give this a try.

MAKES 1 LITRE

150g raw unsalted almonds
or cashew nuts

1_ Place the nuts in a bowl and cover with water, then leave to soak for 2–4 hours (the time required depends on how powerful your blender is). Drain the nuts through a sieve, then give them a rinse under cold water.

2_ Place the nuts in a blender (a high-speed blender is ideal for this) with 1 litre of fresh water and blitz for 1–2 minutes until there are no visible pieces of nut.

3_ Place a piece of muslin or a nut bag over a bowl and pour in the milk to strain, squeezing it gently to extract all the milk.

4_ Transfer the milk to a sterilized glass bottle and keep in the fridge for up to 4 days.

- This milk can be frozen for up to 3 months in an airtight container (not glass).
- Try adding a little honey and unsweetened cocoa powder for chocolate milk.
- Try a hot chai using 500ml warm nut milk, ½ teaspoon ground turmeric, ¼ teaspoon ground cinnamon, ¼ teaspoon ground cardamom and a little honey.

Oat milk

Oat milk has become a popular dairy alternative which you can thank Sweden for, as this is where it originated. Cheaper brands can have an unusual ingredient list, including seed oils, chicory root fibre, stabilizers (gums) and maltodextrin. Manufacturers also use digestive enzymes (alpha amylase) to break down the starch in oats to simple sugars like maltose, which is why it has a sweeter taste. Try making your own natural version made from just oats and water. Don't blitz it too much in the food processor; the heat from the processor will lead it to release starches and develop a slimy consistency. Using very cold water can help avoid this.

MAKES 750ML

100g porridge oats
750ml chilled water

1_ Tip the oats into a food processor or blender and add the water. Blitz for 30 seconds until there are no oats visible.

2_ Place a piece of cheesecloth or muslin in a sieve set over a bowl and pour in the mixture, then allow it to drip through. Try not to squeeze the cloth as this can leave you with slightly slimy oat milk.

3_ Discard the oats and pour the oat milk back into the food processor or blender. Drape the cloth back over the sieve then pour the oat milk through again to strain for a second time.

4_ Transfer the oat milk to a glass jar or jug with a lid and keep in the fridge.

- Homemade oat milk will keep in the fridge for up to 3 days.
- You can add a teaspoon of honey or 1 date when you blitz the oats to add a little sweetness, and 2 tablespoons cocoa powder for chocolate milk.
- This oat milk does not heat well and will not froth.

Sauces, Dressings & Milks

Vegetable stock

Like all ultra-processed foods, the reason we use stock cubes is for convenience, but they never really taste that great or natural. Being prepared and organized in the kitchen is an essential part of living an unprocessed life. Make your stock in large batches and freeze in small containers or even ice-cube trays, which you can just pop into dishes as they cook.

MAKES 1 LITRE

1 large onion, quartered
2 carrots, cut into chunks
2 leeks, cut into chunks
3 celery sticks, cut into chunks
2 garlic cloves, smashed
1 bay leaf
Bunch of flat-leaf parsley (15g)
1 sprig of thyme
½ tsp black peppercorns
½ tsp sea salt

1_ Put all the ingredients into a large saucepan, add 2 litres of water and bring to the boil. Reduce the heat and gently simmer for 2 hours.
2_ Pour the stock through a sieve into a clean container, then leave to cool.

• Stock can be kept in the fridge for 7 days and frozen for 6 months in an airtight container; you can also freeze in ice-cube trays; once frozen, pop out into a resealable freezer bag.

Chicken stock

Making chicken stock should become habitual after a Sunday roast or whenever you cook a whole chicken or boned pieces – just remember before the carcass ends up in the bin. Freeze your stock in small containers for convenience. The little effort this involves is really worth it as you'll always have a batch ready to go.

MAKES 1 LITRE

1kg chicken carcasses
1 large onion, quartered
1 carrot, cut into chunks
1 leek, cut into chunks
1 celery stick, cut into chunks
2 garlic cloves, smashed
1 bay leaf
Bunch of parsley (15g)
1 sprig of thyme
½ tsp black peppercorns
½ tsp sea salt

1_ Put all the ingredients into a large saucepan, add 2 litres of water and bring to the boil. Reduce the heat and gently simmer for 3 hours, occasionally skimming off any froth that comes to the surface.
2_ Pour the stock through a sieve into a clean container, then leave to cool.

• Stock can be kept in the fridge for 7 days and frozen for up to 3 months in an airtight container. You can also freeze this stock in ice-cube trays; once frozen, pop out into a resealable freezer bag.

References

Chassaing, B., et al., 'Dietary Emulsifiers Directly Alter Human Microbiota Composition and Gene Expression Ex Vivo Potentiating Intestinal Inflammation'. *Gut*, 2017; 66(8), 1414–1427.

Delpino, F. M., et al., 'Ultra-Processed Food and Risk Of Type 2 Diabetes: A Systematic Review and Meta-Analysis of Longitudinal Studies'. *International Journal of Epidemiology*, 2022; 51(4), 1120–1141.

Drewnowski A., 'Perspective: Identifying Ultra-Processed Plant-Based Milk Alternatives in the USDA Branded Food Products Database'. *Advances in Nutrition (Bethesda, Md.)*, 2021; 12(6), 2068–2075.

Elizabeth, L., et al., 'Ultra-Processed Foods and Health Outcomes: A Narrative Review'. *Nutrients*, 2020; 12(7), 1955.

Fiolet, T., et al., 'Consumption of Ultra-Processed Foods and Cancer Risk: Results From Nutrinet-Santé Prospective Cohort'. *BMJ (Clinical research ed.)*, 2018; 360, k322.

Gearhardt, A. et al., 'Social, clinical, and policy implications of ultra-processed food addiction'. *BMJ (Clinical research ed.)*, 383, 2023; e075354.

Gomes Gonçalves, N., et al., 'Association Between Consumption of Ultraprocessed Foods and Cognitive Decline'. *JAMA Neurology*, 2023; 80(2), 142–150.

Hall, K. D., et al., 'Ultra-Processed Diets Cause Excess Calorie Intake and Weight Gain: An Inpatient Randomized Controlled Trial of Ad Libitum Food Intake'. *Cell Metabolism*, 2019; 30(1), 67–77.e3.

Lane, M. M., et al., 'Ultraprocessed Food And Chronic Noncommunicable Diseases: A Systematic Review And Meta-Analysis of 43 Observational Studies'. *Obesity Reviews: An Official Journal of the International Association for the Study of Obesity*, 2021; 22(3), e13146.

Ley, R. E., et al., 'Microbial Ecology: Human Gut Microbes Associated with Obesity'. *Nature*, 2006; 444(7122), 1022–1023.

Li, H., et al., 'Association of Ultraprocessed Food Consumption With Risk of Dementia: A Prospective Cohort Study'. *Neurology*, 2022; 99(10), e1056–e1066.

Miclotte, L., & Van de Wiele, T. (2020). 'Food Processing, Gut Microbiota and The Globesity Problem'. *Critical Reviews in Food Science And Nutrition*, 2020; 60(11), 1769–1782.

Rico-Campà, A., et al., 'Association Between Consumption of Ultra-Processed Foods and All Cause Mortality: SUN Prospective Cohort Study'. *BMJ (Clinical research ed.)*, 2019; 365, l1949.

Schnabel, L., et al., 'Association Between Ultra-Processed Food Consumption and Functional Gastrointestinal Disorders: Results From the French NutriNet-Santé Cohort'. *The American Journal of Gastroenterology*, 2018; 113(8), 1217–1228.

Srour, B., at al., 'Dietary Exposure to Nitrites and Nitrates In Association with Type 2 Diabetes Risk: Results From the Nutrinet-Santé Population-Based Cohort Study'. *PLoS Medicine*, 2023; 20(1), e1004149.

Srour, B., et al., 'Ultra-Processed Food Intake and Risk of Cardiovascular Disease: Prospective Cohort Study (Nutrinet-Santé)'. *BMJ (Clinical Research ed.)*, 2019; 365, l1451.

Valdes, A. M., et al., 'Role of the Gut Microbiota in Nutrition And Health'. *BMJ (Clinical Research ed.)*, 2018; 361, k2179.

Index